CUT THE CRAP AND CLOSE THE GAP

CUT THE CRAP
AND
CLOSE THE GAP

THE URGENCY OF
DELIVERING DESIRED RESULTS

JIM COLEMAN

NEW YORK

NASHVILLE • MELBOURNE • VANCOUVER

CUT THE CRAP AND CLOSE THE GAP
THE URGENCY OF DELIVERING DESIRED RESULTS

Published in New York, New York, by Morgan James Publishing. Morgan James is a trademark of Morgan James, LLC. www.MorganJamesPublishing.com

The Morgan James Speakers Group can bring authors to your live event. For more information or to book an event visit The Morgan James Speakers Group at www.TheMorganJamesSpeakersGroup.com.

ISBN 978-1-68350-273-9 paperback
ISBN 978-1-68350-274-6 eBook
Library of Congress Control Number: 2016916270

Cover Design by:
Chris Treccani
www.3dogdesign.net

Interior Design by:
Bonnie Bushman
The Whole Caboodle Graphic Design

In an effort to support local communities, raise awareness and funds, Morgan James Publishing donates a percentage of all book sales for the life of each book to Habitat for Humanity Peninsula and Greater Williamsburg.

Get involved today! Visit
www.MorganJamesBuilds.com

DEDICATION

Momma, you gave me life and unconditional love; you affirmed my potential and inspired me to do great things.

Daddy, you gave me strength and the foundation to be a good man, to never give up, to work hard and to be responsible.

Your eternal spirits continue to live in my heart and guide me every day. Writing this book has been a part of my healing process from the pain I still feel from losing you to heaven.

I will continue your good work while I am alive, so at the end of my journey, God may reward me with the opportunity to see you both again in heaven.

TABLE OF CONTENTS

ACKNOWLEDGMENTS

Cut the Crap and Close the Gap: The Urgency of Delivering Results is not a one-person project. From the beginning, it has been a total team effort with David Hancock, founder of Morgan James Publishing, and Margo Toulouse, managing editor at Morgan James. The Morgan James team provided the support, direction, and encouragement I needed to fulfill a life's dream of writing a book and sharing my thoughts, ideas, and experiences with the world.

I want to thank the late Dr. James Cheek, former president of Howard University, for favorably responding to my mother's plea that Howard's Admissions Department reverse its decision to reject my admission to the university. Gaining admittance to Howard represented a turning point in my life and provided a game-changing opportunity to obtain a formal education in economics, as well as to meet my college sweetheart, Cathy Lynne Clash, and my best friends till this day, nearly forty years later: Rushern L. Baker III, Cissy Beverly, Mike Smart, Richard

Chaney, David Byrd, Billy Marshall, Grant Walker, Rodney Bell, Chuckie Perry, and Michelle Clopton.

I thank my sister, Ruth Coleman, for encouraging me at an early age to study hard so I would gain admittance to Howard. Ruth is an extraordinary role model and a fascinating trailblazer. She became the first woman and the first African American to receive a bachelor's degree in civil engineering from the University of Kentucky. Later in her career she became a professional engineer, a cherished credential in the civil engineering field. Ruth will always be the wind beneath my wings.

I thank my dear cousins Dr. Stanford J. Coleman Jr., his wife, Paula and their daughters Salaam and Dahomey as well as my other dear cousins, Trish and Harvey Hankins and their sons Ivan and Darryl, for their unconditional love and support they provided me while I attended Howard University. I would have dropped out of Howard during the difficult days if I did not have access to the love and encouragement of my dear cousins.

I thank Mr. Jeffery A. Parker, who recruited me to Oscar Mayer & Company. He took a risk by inviting me to Oscar Mayer's headquarters in Madison, Wisconsin, to interview for a corporate job that exceeded my academic and professional credentials. Mr. Parker saw something in me that others didn't, and he gave me the chance of a lifetime.

A special thanks to my spiritual leader, Rev. Dr. W. Franklyn Richardson, senior pastor of Grace Baptist Church in Mount Vernon, New York, and to his son, the Rev. W. Franklyn Richardson III, who has become my third brother and trusted confidante.

I thank RoseMarie Panio, former chair of the Westchester County Republican Party, for encouraging me to run for the New York State Assembly. While I lost the election to a well-deserving incumbent, I won the opportunity to serve the public and do good work for my neighbors in Westchester County, New York, providing me the foundation for a long-term career in public service.

I've been writing this book for the last forty-five years, starting when I was just twelve years old. I hope you find it to be a good story filled with innovative, practical ideas and unconventional, battle-tested solutions to improve the performance of any business. It includes a love story between a mother and her son and a story about a hardworking father of five who bravely tackled giants every day of his life.

This story celebrates the jewel of our American economy, the family farm, and how families leverage the value of their land and livestock production to achieve desired results and generational wealth. And finally, it's a story about how some of America's finest global corporations manage and deliver long-term profitability and why others have simply faded away into the history books.

This book allows me to share with millions of people around the world the extraordinary practical advice I've received over the last forty-five years from my parents, hundreds of highly accomplished Fortune 500 executives, innovative entrepreneurs, and elected officials. Their patient and supportive advice led to my personal success, from being a Kentucky farm boy, to reaching Wall Street as an executive, to being a leader in economic development in two of America's most prosperous counties.

I achieved the American Dream early in my life, and I'm still chasing it in search of the next chapter of serving others, making a bigger impact and leaving a legacy that my parents would be proud of. America offers an abundance of unlimited opportunities. I've learned that the American Dream is real and that America remains the world's best hope for prosperity for the common man and woman.

I purchased my first home at the age of twenty-five in Lanham, Maryland. I became a senior executive in a large Fortune 500 global corporation by the time I was thirty-eight. I acquired millions of dollars in real estate by the time I was forty three, and I've been an economic development leader in two prosperous counties, positively impacting the lives of real people and the business community.

All of my personal accomplishments have been achieved because I embraced the precious wisdom and advice of my parents and the many generous Fortune 500 executives, elected officials, and pastors who've mentored me and, at times, tolerated my deficiencies and weaknesses and made me a better man.

Cut the Crap and Close the Gap offers a management approach and a practical guide for success on how farmers, small business owners, executives, and managers, as well as not-for-profit executive directors, can exceed desired operating results for their organizations. It's filled with a wide selection of stories that are linked to practical advice and key learnings that can be applied to any situation by the reader.

This book is also a great operating guide for parents because it is full of battle-tested ideas from my mother, Cleo, whom I called "Cupcakes," and my father, Sam, on how to develop a child into a successful adult.

Lastly, this book is intended to be a gift of inspiration to anyone who is battling an illness, whether physical or mental, or simply facing life's toughest giants.

Growing up in a Kentucky farm community called Uttingertown made me who I am today. My mother's father, James Russell Johnson, whom I am named after, always used to say, "We are who we are by the time we are five years old. All that happens from the age of five is that we get a little taller and our vocabulary increases by about 100 words, but changing anyone after five years old is nearly impossible."

From being appointed by my father to be the manager of our family farm at the early age of twelve, to attending and graduating from Howard University, receiving a formal education in economics, to working for four Fortune 500 companies that have invested millions of dollars into my professional development, to being a leader for economic development in two vibrant municipalities, I still rely on the principles I learned as a little boy growing up in Uttingertown.

I hope you enjoy this book. I hope it encourages you to aggressively pursue your dreams and to keep on working toward your desired level of personal and professional success.

FOREWORD

Cut the Crap and Close the Gap by Jim Coleman is a fascinating story about the quest to achieve the American Dream through persistence, seizing the moment and pure audacity.

This exciting book also illustrates the "power of one" with Jim's great grandfather, James Coleman, who had the foresight to purchase a farm in Kentucky back in 1888 which later financed the college education of over 300 of his descendants over the next 129 years, including the author's college education at Howard University.

Jim Coleman is a results oriented, high energy motivational speaker and sales and marketing professional who transformed lives and delivered profitable business results during his entire career.

Cut the Crap and Close the Gap is a practical operating guide for farmers, small business owners, executives, managers, sales professionals, auctioneers and anyone else who seeks to achieve the American Dream."

—John S. Nicholls,
National Auctioneers Association President

INTRODUCTION

ARE YOU LEADING THE PACK OR CHASING THE HERD?

- Is your company beating last year's gross sales and net profit results?
- Is your company achieving its annual sales revenue and net profit objectives?
- Are your company's gross sales and net profit growth outperforming your competitors'?
- Are your sales representatives performing better than other sales representatives in your industry?
- Is your company's share of visible space at retail better than your share of market?
- Is your company's profit per share growing faster than your industry?
- Are your company's managers more productive than other managers in your industry?

If you answered "no" to any of these questions, it's time to "cut the crap and close the gap"!

According to Dun & Bradstreet, 585,000 of the more than 22 million small- to medium-sized business in America close each year. Businesses with fewer than twenty employees have only a 37 percent chance of surviving for four years and only a 9 percent chance of surviving for ten years. Nine out of ten business failures are caused by a lack of general business management skills, including management of staff, operations, sales, marketing, and planning.

According to *Fortune* magazine, 10 percent of Fortune 500 companies lost money in 2015 with twenty of these companies losing $1 billion in 2014 and four of them losing more than $10 billion. Rana Foroohar of *Time* magazine writes, "The new Fortune 500 list shows that overall growth for big business stalled in the last year (2015), with profits dropping 11% for firms on the list."

According to Mark J. Perry, a scholar at American Enterprise Institute and a professor of economics and finance at the University of Michigan's Flint campus, "Comparing the Fortune 500 companies in 1955 to the Fortune 500 in 2014, there are **only 61 companies that appear in both lists**. In other words, only 12.2% of the Fortune 500 companies in 1955 were still on the list 59 years later in 2014, and almost 88% of the companies from 1955 have either gone bankrupt, merged, or still exist but have fallen from the top Fortune 500 companies (ranked by total revenues). Most of the companies on the list in 1955 are unrecognizable, forgotten companies today (e.g. Armstrong Rubber, Cone Mills, Hines Lumber, Pacific Vegetable Oil, and Riegel Textile)."

Perry goes on to say, "That's a lot of churning and creative destruction, and it's probably safe to say that almost all of today's Fortune 500 companies will be replaced by new companies in new industries over the next 59 years, and for that we should be thankful. The constant turnover in the Fortune 500 is a positive sign of the dynamism and innovation that characterizes a vibrant consumer-oriented market economy and that dynamic turnover is speeding up in today's hyper-competitive global economy."

Performance gaps between desired results and actual results are often caused by management's resistance to implement bold, innovative, and disruptive strategies or corrective actions that would help their company exceed desired objectives and outperform the market for the long term. As a result, many companies fall victim to the onslaught of newer, smaller disruptive market players who are faster, more innovative, and fiercer and operate at much lower operating costs. These smaller players also provide improved access to consumers and clients that market leaders have written off.

While working for several business units and organizations during the last thirty-four years, I have gained firsthand insight into how successful companies and organizations achieve desired results. It happens when the senior leadership effectively communicates the mission of the enterprise to all frontline employees, including sales representatives, manufacturing employees, and employees in administrative functions, like finance and human resources. Furthermore, it happens when senior management effectively monitors performance metrics and keeps the entire organization informed of its performance level at all times.

Even in professional sports, where everyone on the team is paid generous salaries, is a star, and wears the same kind of uniform and gear, the teams that make it to the playoffs and become the national champions are led by a demanding, deliberate, focused, forward-thinking, and innovative coach who keeps a keen eye on performance metrics and has a low tolerance for poor performance and excuses.

From my days of being a business consultant in New York City, I found that most employees in small and large companies are uninformed about their organization's strategic mission and objectives. Furthermore, many companies don't have an effective employee feedback loop that would allow management to receive constructive feedback and innovative ideas from their employees that could positively impact the company's performance.

The *Cut the Crap and Close the Gap* management approach assumes that strong, strategic, deliberate management leads to desired results and that weak management leads to poor results. Furthermore, this approach focuses on bottom-line results and continuous improvement, where the CEO or business owner promotes a culture where every employee, from top executive down to the janitor, is empowered and responsible for delivering individual performance objectives that contribute to the company's overall performance.

Furthermore, this management approach is based on the intense desire to exceed desired results, with a sharp focus on key performance indicators and metrics that are designed to beat market competitors and change the rules in a given industry. It offers a committed focus on the rapid delivery of quantifiable, game-changing performance metrics, flawless market execution, and low-cost operations. Desired performance levels can include double-digit growth in projected revenue and profits, quantum improvement in organizational productivity, and exceeding the performance of industry competitors.

The *Cut the Crap and Close the Gap* management approach requires that a CEO, business owner, executive, or manager knows the status of his company's performance at all times and is always proactive in taking the necessary steps to prevent and close existing performance gaps. This management approach means preventing and not tolerating performance gaps and deciding to take, by any means necessary, immediate action to prevent and close the gaps whenever and wherever they exist.

At the heart of this management approach is a deep disdain for delayed action, combined with intense impatience and an insatiable desire for innovation and disruption that leads to record growth in revenues and profits. It requires an uncompromising focus and continuous flow of bold and unvarnished assessment of reality and being committed to developing and taking the necessary steps to prevent performance gaps and to immediately eliminate those gaps when they arise.

This management approach requires business owners and managers to be free from conventional wisdom, short-term fixes and tradition and to be willing to aggressively deploy unconventional, innovative and often disruptive strategies and tactics to close performance gaps and exceed desired performance. It requires business owners and managers to think beyond their current understanding and knowledge about their industry and their company's potential, and it challenges them to undertake a journey of breakthrough improvement. It drives executives and managers to operate with "zero gravity," a way of operating without the knowledge of historical barriers and distracting excuses. It's about questioning and challenging conventional wisdom and operating with a spirit of continuous improvement and a willingness to work hard and to work smart.

During the last thirty-four years of my career, I have worked for the best corporations on the planet and have had a front-row seat to some of the finest CEOs and executives in action, delivering record results, including those at Oscar Mayer & Company, Pepsi-Cola Company, Altria, and American Express. These great American companies are market leaders in their industries and are led by talented and innovative CEOs and managers who are committed to continuous improvement. Furthermore, the management teams of these great companies establish high-performance operating cultures that consistently deliver desired business results.

I have personally witnessed the most brilliant senior executives in Fortune 500 companies plan, execute, and transform the performance of their organizations and meet conflicting objectives. These companies compete in very tough, competitive industries where one share point is equivalent to more than $500 million in sales revenue. These great companies hire and retain the best managers and leaders in the world to run their business units, and they expect them to exceed planned financial objectives each quarter and each year. Furthermore, these great companies hold their managers accountable, and managers are quickly removed from these organizations when they fail to meet desired objectives. Each of these great companies holds their management teams accountable to a set of core management responsibilities that include providing clear direction to the organization, effectively allocating precious resources, keeping their entire organization informed about the overall performance of the company versus its annual plan, and building long-term, individual, and organizational capabilities.

In the following chapters, I will illustrate examples of the *Cut the Crap and Close the Gap* management approach I learned as a youngster while I managed my family's small farm in Kentucky. This management approach has carried me to professional and personal success throughout my life. I will also share insights into my key learnings and experiences at the large and small firms where I have been employed over the last thirty-four years.

CHAPTER 1

THE MAKING OF A KENTUCKY GENTLEMAN

Cut the Crap Principle 1: There's no excuse for
failure because we can always do things better.

hile my parents, grandfather, aunts, and uncles usually
voted for Democrats, they were staunch conservatives
in their approach to life. My parents were intolerant

of excuses for poor performance or poor behavior. On many occasions, I witnessed them finding creative ways to solve their personal problems and challenges, and I have seen other people face the same problems and challenges and simply give up.

My parents taught me that most of life's problems are within our control to resolve and that it is our personal responsibility to do so. My mother made me gentle, and my father made me a man.

My mother was a saint. She was the most beautiful woman in the world. She used to claim that she was a softy with a tender heart, especially for underdogs; however, she was clearly not a pushover. She was a combination of steel, resilience, and perseverance. She never gave up on herself, and she never gave up on me. She was a good listener, and she was nonjudgmental of others, no matter what they experienced in their lives. She was a natural caretaker, counselor, social worker, and therapist.

For years, my mother worked all day at Eastern State Hospital, a large psychiatric hospital in Lexington, Kentucky, only to return home in the evening to prepare dinner for her family and then accept pressing, late-night phone calls from other women and friends. These callers were fighting giants in their lives, including bipolar disorder, alcoholism, poverty, physical abuse, and depression.

My father always believed that every healthy, grown man needed to be responsible and accountable to himself and his family, not a burden on his community, country, friends, or family. His favorite saying was, "If you can't find a good job, plant a tree. Do something to make a difference, but for God's sake, get a job and don't be lazy." My father believed that "most people in this world are simply lazy and too ornery to change their ways." He always thought that things could be done better. He was an early adopter and pioneer of the *Cut the Crap and Close the Gap* management approach. He was clearly a process-improvement trailblazer as early as 1950, ten years before I was even born. This is why I strongly embrace this management approach today.

After receiving training on the *Cut the Crap and Close the Gap* approach from my father for the first twenty-nine years of my life, I became obsessed with process improvement and closing performance gaps in my personal and professional life. Even when I completed my chores on our family farm, like feeding the hogs, spreading manure over our fields, cleaning up the barn, parking the pickup truck and tractor in the barn for the night, or when I got an B in a difficult subject in school or perfectly played "At the Cross" on our family piano, my father would still say, "Is that the best you can do? There's always room for improvement." At the time, I thought my father was just being unfair to me, but today, though he's been in heaven since 1989, I still respond to his guidance, and I even hear his voice saying there's always room for improvement.

My father beat the odds all his life. He lost his mother, Mollie Coleman, who died at age fifty-two in 1933, when he was only ten years old. Right after her funeral, he had to be a little man. He became the caretaker for his youngest sister, Anna, and he had to care for his father, who was suffering from loneliness, depression caused by losing his wife, and alcoholism. My father deeply mourned the loss of his mother for next fifty-nine years of his life. He was overwhelmed by a sense of abandonment, saying often, "My mother died on me when I was ten years old." While I never met my father's mother, I somehow joined him in this mourning process. It impacted my own life and created in me a difficulty in accepting deep loss and abandonment, too. I even miss Mollie Coleman till this very day, and I'm still sad she died at such an early age.

In his early twenties, the United States Army drafted my father into service, and he was sent off to fight the Nazis in Italy during World War II. He faced a fierce enemy that sent massive fire, bullets, and bombs his way, but he survived. After his service, he returned to an American society that did not honor his service but rather mistreated him because of the color of his black skin. Through it all, my father remained focused and did not allow this injustice to blow out the candle in his life. Till the day he died, he stayed focused on seizing the moment that was available for him and his family in America.

My father, who was born during the Great Depression, believed that walking away from a problem was never acceptable. He'd lost his childhood the day he lost his mother, and as a result, he was a grown man for fifty-nine of his sixty-nine years. He had an intense disdain for anyone who was not willing to embrace responsibility. As a result of facing a challenging life at a very young age, he developed the divine gift of being a problem solver. He was obsessed about closure and bottom-line results, solving difficult problems, and protecting and providing for his family. Maybe this is why his young heart gave out at the early age of sixty-nine.

My father was an incredible multitasker—a farmer, a postal mail carrier, and a waiter at private parties that were hosted in the homes of prominent, multimillionaire Kentucky horse breeders. He graduated with a bachelor's degree in agriculture from Kentucky State University, but at the end of the day, the best job in Lexington, Kentucky, for an educated black man was being a mail carrier for the United States Postal Service.

Of all the jobs my father had, he enjoyed being a waiter at the big, private parties. That's where he earned a special master's degree in business administration from prominent Kentucky horse breeders and successful businessmen, like Mr. Leslie Combs, owner of the great Spendthrift Farm of Lexington.

According to *New York Times* journalist Thomas Rogers, "Spendthrift Farm, which Mr. Combs bought in 1936 with a $600,000 inheritance and proceeds from selling an insurance agency he had founded in West Virginia, enjoyed early prosperity and grew from 126 acres to 6,000.

"After World War II, Mr. Combs revitalized the practice of syndicating stallions, beginning with Beau Pere, whom he syndicated to 20 investors for $5,000 each. He later syndicated such champion thoroughbreds as Nashua, Majestic Prince and Raise a Native."

Furthermore, Thomas wrote, "Spendthrift, named for a famous racehorse owned by Mr. Combs's great-grandfather, was once the home of Seattle Slew and Affirmed, the Triple Crown winners of 1977 and 1978, and the farm may have reached its peak in stallion syndication in 1978, when those two champions were syndicated for $12 million and $16 million, respectively."

According to my father's many stories, Mr. Combs seemed to be very determined to achieve perfection, profit, and success in his horse breeding business. My father always told me stories about how he was teased by the other waiters during Mr. Combs's private parties for being what they called "Spendthrift Farm's Biggest Uncle Tom."

Mr. Combs would often rely on my father's advice in dealing with a given prospective buyer of his young thoroughbreds. My father would always tell the story about how Mr. Combs would almost come to tears after receiving a large, six-figure check from a wealthy international buyer of one of his thoroughbreds. Mr. Combs would turn to my father and ironically say, "Coleman, they stealing all of Cousin Les's ponies today. Cousin Les is barely making a dime."

At one of Spendthrift's big parties, Mr. Combs listened in to one of the regular teasing sessions that was conducted by my father's colleagues, who were fellow waiters, about my father being "Spendthrift Farm's Biggest Uncle Tom." When Mr. Combs had heard enough, he quickly entered the kitchen and said, "Coleman is not Spendthrift Farm's Biggest Uncle Tom. I am Spendthrift Farm's Biggest Uncle Tom. And if Coleman and I stop Uncle Tomming, none of us will be working."

My father often told me another Spendthrift story about how he personally welcomed former California Governor and Mrs. Ronald Reagan into Spendthrift's mansion for a requested private meeting with Mr. Combs shortly after the Kentucky Derby. Apparently, Governor Reagan had approached Mr. Combs during the derby and asked if he could stop by the farm later to discuss purchasing any of his retired horses for his ranch in California. According to my father, after he settled Governor and Mrs. Reagan down in the living room with refreshments, he went upstairs to inform Mr. Combs that his important guests had arrived and were anxiously waiting to meet with him. Mr. Combs continued to talk on the phone long distance with New York bankers and other syndicate investment partners about the concerns related to the operations at Spendthrift. After more than an hour had passed while Mr. Combs remained on the phone, Governor and Mrs. Reagan decided to leave.

When Mr. Combs finally came downstairs, he was astonished to find that the Reagans had been too impatient to wait and had left. "Where are Ronnie and Nancy?" he asked my father. My father informed him that the Reagans had left because they felt they had been treated disrespectfully. According to my father, Mr. Combs shot back, "Forget'em. They wanted my ponies for nothing."

Spendthrift Farm was a success because Leslie Combs managed his farm with a very deliberate, focused management style, combined with his seductive, Kentucky gentlemanly selling skills. Combs was ahead of his time when it came to syndicate financing in the horse business. He used innovative syndicated financing models that other breeding farms were not using. These models led to Spendthrift's global success in producing winning thoroughbreds.

As my father would explain, Combs was maniacally focused on profitable results. Movie stars, elected officials, and anyone else who could not pay full, premium prices for his horses or help him meet his own personal and business objectives did not impress him. Business was personal with Combs. He would even make that clear to my father when he would see him serving his family members during a big horse sale instead of paying greater attention to prospective customers who were ready to pay full, six-figure prices for Spendthrift's thoroughbreds. Combs once told my father, "Coleman, remember to always take care of our paying guests first and let my family get their own drinks. My family is as po' as me. Dealing with po' people will break you. As long as you live, always deal with your equals or your superiors because po' people will break you!"

Combs was an early adopter and professor of the *Cut the Crap and Close the Gap* management approach. My father greatly admired Combs's ruthless but gentlemanly style, and he embraced and deployed Combs's aggressive, deliberate, results-oriented, impatient management approach in how he managed our farm, Coleman Crest, his family, and his own life.

My parents made me a Kentucky gentleman in the likes of Sam Coleman and Leslie Combs—proud, fierce, deliberate, impatient, sensitive, kindhearted, generous, tough, focused, resourceful, and never a quitter. This has enabled me to survive personal and professional setbacks, as well as to thrive in all my endeavors over the last forty-five years of my life.

CLOSE THE GAP TAKEAWAYS:

- We have the power to choose between being a victim or being an active participant in the American free enterprise system.
- We have the power to eliminate or provide access to the right people in our lives.

- No matter how difficult life can get, we can always focus on the controllables in our lives to achieve desired results.
- Successful people are deliberate and focused; very few people achieve desired results through luck.
- Carefully choosing your friends is important; we are the average of our five best friends.

CHAPTER 2

SEIZING THE MOMENT

Cut the Crap Principle 2:
It's always darkest before the dawn.

My ancestors were kidnapped from western Africa. They didn't travel to America on a passenger ship like the Mayflower. Passenger ships were reserved for other immigrants who were headed to America to discover freedom from burdensome government and to claim a new beginning and new opportunities. According to my family's verbal historian, Uncle Sam D. Coleman, my grandfather's brother, my ancestors crossed the Atlantic on a slave ship headed for Spotsylvania, Virginia, only to discover slavery, oppression, and torture upon arrival.

When my ancestors arrived in Spotsylvania, there was no fanfare or well-wishers waiting to greet them at the dock. There were no photographers to take their pictures and no special transportation to take them to their final destination in the New World. What awaited them was a job that had no pay, crops to raise without adequate tools, and broken down, crumbling shacks, at best, for shelter.

Of course, "Coleman" was not my ancestors' original name. Their African name was left at the docks of western Africa, and to this day, I still do not know my original African surname. Uncle Sam used to tell my mother all the time, "Cleo, we were Duersons before we were Colemans, and I don't know why." I recently connected the dots of Uncle Sam's account of our history by discovering that my ancestors were given the name Duerson because they had been purchased upon their arrival to America by a wealthy family in Spotsylvania called the Duersons.

From what I have put together from the available information, combined with Uncle Sam's recitation of our history, it is believed that my ancestors' owners were John and Nellie Duerson. John and Nellie had five children: Thomas, Maria, Salina, John, and Mary. Mary left Spotsylvania and relocated to Fayette County, Kentucky (Lexington), in the late 1700s. She took several slaves with her, and they are believed to be my ancestors. When Mary arrived in Kentucky, she met and married a man named Coleman, and when her last name changed from Duerson to Coleman, so did my ancestor's last name change to Coleman.

My great-grandfather James Coleman and his parents were slaves on a farm in Uttingertown, a small town eight miles from Lexington. My great-grandfather and his parents and siblings raised crops and livestock. They worked hard in the fields and in the kitchens for their slave owners. They closely observed how their wealthy slavemasters would leverage the value of their land to finance the purchase of farm equipment, supplies, and the education of their children. Much of the knowledge they picked up through observation and listening while serving their master's dinner, they later employed to purchase property and change the lives of future generations.

According to research conducted by Kentucky Education Television (KET), "As the conflict over slavery heated up in the early 1800s, many abolitionists hoped that removing former slaves to Africa would further their cause by eliminating the need for whites and freed blacks to live and work together (a possibility only radicals entertained at the time). Some slaveholders were troubled by the morality of slavery and wanted to free their slaves—but only if the former slaves could then be sent far away. Meanwhile, other slaveholders who had no intention of relinquishing their own slaves supported the removal of those already freed because they saw the freedmen as economic competitors and potential leaders of a slave revolt. Whites representing all of these viewpoints came together in the American Colonization Society (ACS), though the alliance was always uneasy. The society's founders included Kentucky statesman Henry Clay, a slave owner himself who favored emancipation in theory but advocated a conservative, gradual approach."

KET's research continued, "In 1821, the ACS purchased land in Africa to found the colony of Liberia ("land of the free"). A Kentucky state affiliate was formed in 1828, and the members began to raise money for transporting Kentucky blacks—free volunteers as well as slaves set free on the condition that they agree to emigrate—to Africa. In its three decades of existence, the Kentucky Colonization Society managed to send only about 650 people to Africa. But the society did raise enough money to buy a 40-square-mile site along the St. Paul's River—Kentucky in Africa. The principal town, established in 1846, was named Clay-Ashland, in honor of Clay and his Lexington estate, Ashland."

In hopes of returning to freedom and escaping the harsh torture that many blacks faced in America, many of my ancestors returned to Liberia near the end of slavery. To begin their departure from Kentucky to Liberia, they traveled to Cincinnati to catch a small vessel down the Mississippi river to New Orleans. They joined a group of other freed slaves, then left America on a small ship. More than half of the ship's passengers died en route to Liberia.

In 1853, one of my ancestors, William David Coleman of Fayette County, departed the state and came to Liberia at age eleven with his widowed mother. He entered politics in his thirties, serving as a representative, a senator, and vice president, and then succeeded to the presidency in 1896 when Joseph

Cheeseman died in office. He was re-elected to the presidency twice. I now know why I have such a deep affection for politics and why I had such a burning desire to run for the New York State Assembly in 2006.

After searching for my Clay-Ashland, Liberia, relatives for the last fifteen years, on July 15, 2016, I finally met them at an annual Coleman Clay-Ashland family reunion held in Bowie, Maryland. It was fascinating to meet my Liberian relatives and to share stories about our heritage. Amazingly, they had similar facial features and personalities. Clearly, we are all part of the same "Coleman Kentucky Tribe."

Instead of returning to Clay Ashland, Liberia, for what was believed to be a better life that included freedom, resources, and our original culture, my great-grandfather chose to remain in America to build a life for himself and his family in Uttingertown. On March 27, 1888, just twenty-five years after President Abraham Lincoln courageously signed the act to end slavery in America, James Coleman purchased the land that he and his parents had tilled as slaves. With the help of loans from the Union Benevolent Society Lodge #28 and local banks, he purchased the parcel of land which is known today as Coleman Crest Farm. He paid John H. Darnaby and his wife, Mary, $1,200 for the land.

James Coleman and his parents had been slaves on Coleman Crest Farm, and now he was the sole owner of an economic enterprise that would transform the lives of more than 300 of his descendants over the next 129 years. Every time I look at the deed to Coleman Crest, it gives me cold chills to think that a former slave had the vision and somehow discovered an innovative way to purchase land. Today, it would be equivalent to me buying the Empire State Building. The audacity of James Coleman to buy the land he had tilled as a slave is the foundation of my father's and my own personal, deep belief that any goal we attempt to achieve can be met if we are truly committed to it.

During the twenty-two years after the purchase of Coleman Crest, James Coleman raised his family there. He and his wife, Lucy, raised four sons, Sam, George, William, and John (my grandfather), and one daughter, Susie. James's children were the first generation of African Americans who were free and landowners.

James Coleman was a leader in Uttingertown and a respected member and officer in the community church, Uttingertown Baptist Church, and the Union Benevolent Society Lodge #28. He was a very proud man who had the vision and the wisdom to learn from wealthy land owners to acquire and finance land through the production of profitable crops and livestock. Somehow, he kept his sights on prosperity, even in the face of harsh racism and a lack of formal education.

From everything my father told me about James Coleman, he seized the moment by establishing a clear, personal vision of success, and he stayed focused on things he could control, including hard work, saving money, providing discipline and love to his children, maintaining good relationships with creditors, and having a firm belief that his Lord would provide better days ahead for him and his family.

In 1910, after experiencing life as a slave and as a successful land owner and entrepreneur, James Coleman died, leaving Coleman Crest Farm to his sole heirs, who were his children. This included Sam and his wife, Carrie; George and his wife, Myrtle; William and his wife, Effie; Susie and her husband, Earnest Jackson; and John and his wife, Mollie (my grandparents). Upon their deaths, James Coleman and his wife were buried in our family's cemetery on the farm.

All of James Coleman's heirs later transferred their ownership rights to Coleman Crest to my grandfather, John Coleman. While John and Mollie continued to face the severe oppression of segregation, racism, and a very turbulent economy that was in a deep depression, they seized the moment, and they loved building a life for their family on Coleman Crest Farm.

John and Mollie raised seven children, James, Ada, Stanford, Clifton, Ben, Anna, and Samuel. They worked hard to satisfy the needs of their family by effectively managing Coleman Crest. They successfully cared for their children and financed their college educations by raising crops and livestock and selling them to the local markets. They also leveraged the value of Coleman Crest through the acquisition of several loans that were secured by the present value of the farm. Just like James Coleman, John and Mollie were trailblazers who believed in the American Dream and seized all that America had to offer.

During a very difficult time that caused John and Mollie to fall behind on their mortgage payments, the bank decided to foreclose on a $500 loan Coleman Crest had secured. John and Mollie had acquired this loan to send their son Clifton to Morehouse College in Atlanta. Foreclosure on the loan would mean that John and Mollie would lose their ownership of Coleman Crest to the bank.

The bank had decided to foreclose on the loan because John and Mollie were three months behind on their seven-dollar-per-month loan payments. While this may seem like an unbelievably easy amount to pay, paying seven dollars every month in the 1930s was not easy due to the poor economy and the difficulty in generating a profit from the sale of crops and livestock.

When the mortgage banker arrived to inform John and Mollie that their loan was about to be foreclosed, Mollie became visibly shaken and called on her Lord for support. Because of his pride and frustration, John refused to negotiate with the banker. He told Mollie, "I'm not going to beg another white man for anything."

Mollie refused to give up on convincing the banker to not foreclose on their bank loan. Instead of being consumed with pride, she kindly requested the mortgage banker join her in prayer at their kitchen table before proceeding with his conversation concerning foreclosure. Mollie got on her knees and immediately began to pray. She was known in our small church as a very religious woman who believed in the power of prayer. When she was called on to pray in the church, the members were often moved to tears and consumed with the Holy Spirit and emotion. Mollie never hesitated to call on the Lord's help when she faced serious challenges. The foreclosure of Coleman Crest was one of those serious occasions when she felt she had to call on her Lord, and I personally thank God every day that she did!

Speaking in tongues is a common practice in Christian charismatic circles and involves some ecstatic utterance delivered while in a state of religious excitation and, allegedly, while under the influence of the Holy Spirit. A person speaking in tongues might start speaking a human language they could not otherwise know or a "spiritual" language.

Mollie was a practitioner of speaking in tongues when she prayed. She was deeply emotional, and she spoke in religious tongues for the mortgage broker, her family, and for our farm. The mortgage broker was so moved by Mollie's powerful prayer that he responded by saying, "You all are crazy; just get caught up," and with that, he quickly left their home in fear of being placed under a spell by Mollie's spiritual connections to the Lord. The broker never returned to the farm, and Mollie and John later satisfied the note.

Today, as I think back, my life and the lives of more than 300 of James Coleman's direct descendants would be very different if Mollie Coleman had not called upon the support of her Lord through prayer to save Coleman Crest Farm.

By saving the farm and leveraging the value of Coleman Crest through several bank loans and by raising profitable cops and livestock, John and Mollie financed the college education of their children during the Great Depression, the most difficult economic years for our country. Their oldest daughter, Ada, graduated from Kentucky State University with a degree in education and became a teacher in Richmond, Virginia; their son Stanford graduated from Lincoln University and Meharry Medical School and became a medical doctor in Dayton, Ohio; their son Clifton attended Morehouse University; their youngest daughter, Anna, graduated from Kentucky State University with a degree in education and became a teacher; and my father, Sam, graduated from Kentucky State with a degree in agriculture. This is why I am so passionate about helping small business owners build profitability and acquire real estate. Among other reasons, I want to help them provide for their families and send their children and future generations to fine educational institutions.

Mollie's death at age fifty-two resulted from complications related to diabetes and cancer. While her life was cut short from these terrible illnesses and oppression, she left a very powerful contribution to her family and our community. While my father was only ten years old when she died, her spirit was so powerful that I remember him speaking about her almost every day of his life. Many of my father's powerful traits and abilities were directly acquired from the short, precious ten years he had with his mother.

My father's inability to recover from the loss of his mother was not helped when his father quickly rejected an opportunity that would have allowed my father to live in Richmond, Virginia. Following Mollie's funeral, my father's oldest sister, Ada, offered to take him and his sister Anna to Richmond with her to expose them to a great education and new world. When my father's father said no to the offer, it was as if my father had lost the opportunity to travel abroad to go to school in France. He never forgot this, and it often led to uneasy relations between him and his older siblings. My father felt his older siblings had been given opportunities to enjoy a successful life that he and his youngest sister Anna would never experience.

Upon the death of my grandfather, John Coleman, in 1949, my parents became the custodians of Coleman Crest Farm. Replicating the success of John and Mollie, my parents built a brand-new home on the farm in 1950, and they raised their five children, Ruth, Sam, Edward, myself, and Rhetta. We raised corn, tobacco, hay, and a large garden, and we also raised a diverse portfolio of livestock, including cows, hogs, sheep, rabbits, and chickens.

My parents met while they were in college at Kentucky State. My father loved my mother for her beauty, her love for education, and her desire to change the world by helping people who were in need. My mother loved my father for his vision for their future, his gentlemanly ways and his strong confidence.

We lived a fun life on our farm. We enjoyed many family reunions where all my uncles and aunts would return to the farm to celebrate the Fourth of July, Uncle Ben's birthday, and our history. There always seemed to be a lot of love and passion in the air. Even during the many heated debates and arguments my parents waged on everything from politics to college education financing, from the Vietnam War to the family budget, I always learned a lot from them.

James Coleman's decision to stay in America and to purchase Coleman Crest positively impacted the lives of over 300 descendants over the last 129 years. Only in America could an African American family go from being slaves to being college graduates in only two generations. My life would be different if James Coleman had not purchased Coleman Crest. My life today would be very different if my Grandmother Mollie hadn't prayed with the mortgage banker.

Today, I live in an America that is very different from the America my ancestors, including my parents, knew. The America I enjoy offers tremendous opportunity to all of its citizens. In recent years, for example, Barak Obama, an African American, was elected twice by most Americans to be our president.

America provides an incredible life of abundance for its ordinary citizens. Wealthy people can enjoy a great life anywhere in the world, but what separates America from other countries is that America offers a high standard of living for all its citizens. While the news media and politicians during our normal election cycles can sometimes make us feel that America's best days have passed, when, for example, our economy only grows at 1 or 2 percent, America's economy is still second to none in the world. At any given time, more than 96 percent of adult Americans are employed. Most of our streets and neighborhoods are safe. Our banking system is stable and strong. As Americans, we enjoy the rule of law, making contracts between business entities ironclad. We have high-quality standards for the production of the food we consume, the purity of the water we drink, the cleanliness of the air we breathe, and the safety of the cars we drive. And while our healthcare system can always be improved, our standards for healthcare are second to none around the globe.

America is the only country in the world that has an immigration challenge. There are more people around the world who are trying to get into America than those who are trying to leave. And of those who think America is on the wrong path, not one of them is ready to leave in protest.

America offers more opportunity and social mobility than any other country in the world. It is the only country that has a large population of self-made millionaires and billionaires. According to a recent report by CNBC, "Despite volatile financial markets and slow economic growth, the U.S. added

300,000 new millionaires in 2015, bringing the total to a record 10.4 million, according to a new report." What's even more fascinating is that there are 35,000 African-American millionaires in the United States."

Only in America could James Coleman be a slave, and two generations later, his descendants are graduates of major universities, practicing medicine, civil engineering, education, marketing, politics, agriculture, education, television production, mortgage processing, law, and social work and are the sole owners of profitable businesses and prime real estate.

Today, Americans live longer, fuller lives. In 1900, the life expectancy in America was less than fifty years. According to a *USA Today* article and a report by the Centers for Disease Control and Prevention's National Center for Health Statistics, "Life expectancy in the USA rose in 2012 to 78.8 years—a record high. The news is a little better for women, a little worse for men. Life expectancy for females is 81.2 years; for males, it's 76.4 years."

My parents' mothers died in their early fifties. My mother lived until she was seventy-three. This extension of the life span means more years to enjoy life, family, and friends and all that America has to offer.

While I greatly love and admire my Clay-Ashland, Liberia, relatives and the incredible heritage of my people in Liberia, if James Coleman had joined my other ancestors on that vessel down the Mississippi river to New Orleans then across the Atlantic to travel to Liberia, I could have been born into a life with limited opportunity for advancement. I would undoubtedly have married a woman of my identical socioeconomic and religious background. I would almost certainly have become a permanent field laborer. I would have probably socialized only within my immediate tribe. I would have a whole set of opinions and perspectives that could be predicted, and they would not be very different from what my father believed or his father before him. In short, my life would, to a large degree, have been given to me at birth without much opportunity to change or improve it.

In America, my life has taken a radically different course than the one I would have lived for the last fifty-six years in Liberia. I attended college because my parents leveraged a real estate asset called Coleman Crest Farm. Once in college, I started with a major in chemistry and then changed it to economics. I expanded my interest in politics. My political perspective began as a "Johnson Man" (committed Democrat), which is what my father understandably was as a result of the many laws that were passed because of US President Lyndon B. Johnson's leadership. However, as I began to form my own political opinions, I felt the conservative values I had learned from my parents, including hard work, free enterprise, family, personal responsibility, lower taxes, national security, and sacrifice for tomorrow, were more associated with the Republican Party, so I decided to become a "College Republican" while attending Howard University. I had a deep admiration for Ronald Reagan.

My father could not believe it when I told him I respected President Reagan, and I quickly reminded him that he was more conservative than Reagan. I also reminded him that while President Johnson had courageously pushed for civil rights legislation, the passage of this important legislation in Congress was a result of the many Republican senators and congressmen, like George Herbert Walker Bush, who voted for civil rights in the face of many Southern democrats who were staunchly against civil rights.

My political opinions were very rare for a student at Howard since the student body was, and remains, predominantly African American and staunchly Democrat. Ironically, many of the students I met there were raised with and believed in these same conservative values. I concluded that voting Democrat was done mostly out of habit and respect for what President Johnson had successfully achieved for civil rights.

I also enjoyed my studies in economics and marketing, and I decided to have a career as a sales and marketing executive. I married a beautiful, intelligent woman named Cathy Clash, whose ancestry is African and American Indian. In my early twenties, I found myself in a fascinating career as a sales and marketing executive with a major Fortune 500 company, and I was able to purchase and own my first home at age twenty-five in Lanham, Maryland. No other country, I am certain, would have permitted the great-grandson of a slave to work in any large company in its society, own real estate, and become a multimillionaire all within the last fifty-six years.

In most countries around the globe, a person's fate and identity are handed to them at birth. In America, we get to decide our own fate. America is a country where you get to write your own unique story and design your own destiny. I've come to believe that being born in America is like being handed a book with blank pages, and you are the author. This idea of being the author of your own future is very powerful, and it is what makes America so attractive to every citizen of every other country in the world.

While racism, gender inequality, socioeconomic discrimination, police brutality, challenged public school systems, complex healthcare delivery systems, and pay inequity have been and continue to be a problem in America, the country has made enormous efforts to eliminate these problems through important pieces of legislation that have been successfully passed over the last 150 years.

Ultimately, my parents, grandparents, and great-grandparents loved America because, more than any other country, it makes possible the good life for most of its citizens.

My great-grandfather was a slave, but he ended up purchasing a piece of land in Kentucky that continues to finance the college education of his descendants. James Coleman died loving America.

My father fought Hitler's army in the bloody fields of Italy; however, he had to ride in the back of the train and bus to go back home to Kentucky at the end of the war. My father died loving America. My father always had a special way of seeing life and seizing the moment. I guess he formed this skill when he lost his dear mother at the very young age of ten. My father always saw the glass as half full. Even when he faced challenges, he would always say, "It's always darkest before the dawn"— meaning, good times were on the way.

My mother was told she would never get ahead because she did not have a master's degree, so she attended and graduated from the University of Kentucky's College School of Social Work with a master's degree in social work and became the chief social worker at Eastern State Hospital. America was a tough place for her, but she too died loving America.

What my parents and ancestors loved most about America is that the possibility of seizing the moment of a better life for future generations is not a dream but a reality! I am a product of ancestors who seized the moment, and I am committed to helping other people seize the moment and capitalize on all of the opportunities that are available in America.

The *Cut the Crap and Close the Gap* management approach is all about seizing the moment. It's all about refusing to wait for someone else to solve our problems, but rather, operating with an urgent, get it done now attitude because tomorrow is not promised!

CLOSE THE GAP TAKEAWAYS:

- The human spirit can withstand the harshest forms of oppression to achieve desired results.
- In our quest for achieving desired results and a life of abundance, we must focus on the positives that surround us, even during our most difficult times.
- The personal decisions we make today can impact the lives of hundreds of people, including our family members, over the next 100 years.
- In America, we have the power and ability to determine our own reality and our desired level of abundance and success.

CHAPTER 3

DON'T KILL THE GOOSE THAT LAYS THE GOLDEN EGG

Cut the Crap Principle 3: When times get tough, we may need to chart a new course to reach our desired destination, but quitting is not an option.

It was an early August day in 1973. The heat monkeys were jumping all over the front of our pickup truck, our driveway was as dusty as it could be, and a management change was on the horizon at Coleman Crest Farm. Our hogs were hungry and dehydrated as I was watering them at the hog pen and flies were swarming like crazy. Only a few days before, my older brothers, Bubba and Coley, had left the farm to attend college at Kentucky State University and Eastern Kentucky University respectively. During Bubba's and Coley's tenure running the farm for my father, they'd taken care of our livestock and raised the crops. Now all of this was about to become my responsibility.

I'd have to take care of our hogs, cows, sheep, and dogs, and all our farm equipment.

On this hot Kentucky day, Daddy came up to the barn to inform me of my promotion from farmhand to manager of Coleman Crest. Daddy said, with a fierce sense of urgency and intensity, "Bubba and Coley are gone to college, and they aren't coming back to the farm. You're not supposed to come back after you go to college. I need you to take care of the farm, and you are now the manager of Coleman Crest. You seem like you really love the farm. It's gone if you don't hold on to it."

I couldn't believe what my father was saying. Now I was going to be the boss, as well as one day own the farm with the responsibility of preserving it for future generations. I was thrilled with the prospect of what was about to happen. Daddy went on to describe my management compensation plan for my new position. Daddy explained, "As manager of Coleman Crest, you will receive three hots and a flop" (AKA three hot meals and a bed to sleep in), which he made clear was all contingent on the sales results of our livestock and crops. He further explained my deferred bonus: he would pay for my college education if we saved enough money over the next few years and if the bank was willing to give us a loan on the farm when it was time for me to go to college. It didn't take me long to realize I had already been receiving "three hots and a flop" for the past twelve years, but now as manager of Coleman Crest, I would have to earn my three hots and a flop.

When I became the farm manager, Daddy was already fifty years old. He was tired from raising three older children, who were in a different generation than me and my sister Rhetta.

He was also tired from carrying a large mortgage on the farm of $10,000 at a payment of over $100 per month for the ranch house my parent's built on the property. Daddy was also exhausted from thousands of dollars in additional debt from home equity loans to send my oldest sister and two brothers to school; so he had no tolerance left to treat me like I was a twelve-year-old kid.

Daddy talked to me like I was an adult, and I listened to him like I was an adult. I was never spanked or put on some sort of punishment because my parents had no time to issue spankings or punishment—they needed me to deliver on my daily farm chores and to be a grown up at twelve! I embraced Daddy's expectations of me to work hard and to be accountable at managing the farm. Daddy made it clear that I had to do a good job to help him generate enough revenue from the sale of our livestock and tobacco to pay for my brothers' and sister's education and to put away savings for my very own education. Most of all, Daddy wanted me to do a good job so we could generate enough farm income to pay off the farm's debts. Daddy saw how the rich horse farmers would use their farm proceeds and leverage the value of their farms to send their children to college, and he was determined to do the same for all five of his children.

As the new manager of Coleman Crest, I quickly learned how to be resourceful, cut costs, minimize waste, and care for our livestock that relied on me for their survival. Looking back, it was an incredible opportunity for me to be exposed to such a high level of management, leadership, and responsibility at such an early age. I never expected Daddy to tell me how to run the farm. I was in charge, and I did what I thought made sense in real time. I set the course and established objectives and priorities every day on what was important, and I flawlessly executed my chores without having to be reminded by my father about what needed to be done. I was a proud producer, and I was committed to my role as manager of Coleman Crest.

Running Coleman Crest taught me the critical elements of effective management, which are the foundational principles of the *Cut the Crap and Close the Gap* management approach. I learned how to effectively distribute and manage precious resources and time, know the status of the farm's performance at all times, and to always find ways to enhance my understanding of agricultural economics and management skills as a young manager of our farm.

Being the manager showed me that nothing in life is free and that it's unacceptable to not deliver on the expectations of senior management or investors. In the case of running Coleman Crest, the senior manager and sole investor was my father, and the expectation he held me accountable for was to preserve Coleman Crest for future generations.

We raised many forms of livestock, including hogs, sheep, cows, rabbits, and chickens, as well as crops like tobacco, corn, and a big vegetable garden. We literally tried raising a wide array of livestock and crops to generate revenue on Coleman Crest. Daddy was a total capitalist, and he was determined to use every square inch of space on the farm to turn a dollar.

As Coleman Crest's new manager, I loved the responsibility of doing my job well; however, I became frustrated with the challenge of keeping our hogs locked up in their pen to prevent them from rooting our neighbors' fields. Daddy and I tried everything in the world to stop them from breaking out of their pens, including ringing their snouts so it would be too painful for them to lift their pen's fences. Daddy and I also castrated them to reduce their desire to break out of their pens. He served as the surgeon, and I was his assistant. I held the hogs while my father performed the painful surgery. Afterward, I used a broken-handled mop to coat their wound with a good dash of turpentine to kill any form of bacteria that would lead to infection.

Even after ringing their noses and castrating our hogs, they still broke out of their pens. We began receiving 5 a.m. daily phone calls from our neighboring farmers about our roaming hogs. This forced me and Spot, my Dalmatian, to round them up and head them home to their pens before I even had a chance to bathe for school. Out of pure desperation and frustration, I was determined to find a creative solution that would stop our hogs from breaking out of our pens.

While we raised corn for our hogs, there was never enough corn production from our farm to satisfy their insatiable appetites. As a result, we had to purchase additional corn from Southern States, a local grain and livestock feed company in Lexington, to supplement the corn we raised on the farm. Daddy had always monitored our costly supplemental purchases of corn from Southern States, and he had encouraged Bubba and Coley to minimize the portions of Southern States-purchased corn to contain our overall costs. While I understood this cost containment objective, little did it do to resolve the core reason why our hogs were breaking out of our pens and rooting up our neighbors' fields. I concluded that our hogs were escaping because they were flat-out hungry and wanted more to eat.

One day it dawned on me that if I simply doubled the amount of purchased corn from Southern States, our hog's appetite could be satisfied, and that would end the breakouts. I understood that we'd be paying double our current bill for the corn, but I believed, given the circumstances, this was okay because our hogs would be bigger and we could get more for them at the fall livestock sales. So I began implementing my new strategy, and within a few days, our hogs stopped breaking out. Within two months, they were looking fat and full and were ready to be sold for top dollar at the livestock market.

Within three months of the start of my new feed strategy, my father said to me as he inspected our hogs, "Look a yonder. These are the biggest hogs we've ever had." I was excited about his appraisal of my work; however, I braced myself for his customary, "But there's always room for improvement." Like I thought he would, Daddy followed his positive feedback with, "But we've got to do something different. You are going to break us because of all of the extra feed I'm buying from Southern States." I was happy that Daddy realized my hard work had produced the best hogs we'd ever had at Coleman Crest, and I could only imagine that there would be one option he would choose that would prevent us from "going broke": to sell our hogs because it was now costing us too much to produce high-quality, good-looking hogs.

Daddy quickly told me that giving the hogs all of this extra corn was not going to work, and he said, "I'm gonna have to come up with a better idea than buying all of that corn you're feeding the hogs." I replied, "Daddy, why don't we just sell these hogs and stop trying to raise them?" Daddy responded, "Jimmy, you can't sell the goose that lays the golden egg," and with that, he headed to the house for supper. At that time, I did not understand the relationship between preventing our hogs from breaking out of our pen at five in the morning and the goose's golden egg.

A couple of days later, Daddy came back up to the barn to talk to me about his new idea that would prevent us from having to buy all that expensive corn from Southern States. I was still hoping that Daddy's solution would be to completely divest from the hog business. When Daddy finally made it to the pig pen, he was beaming and seemed excited to talk. Daddy explained that he had negotiated an agreement with the Saratoga Restaurant, a large, successful, well-known full-service restaurant in Lexington. The agreement he had negotiated with the Saratoga Restaurant included our commitment to dispose of large barrels of their table scraps three to four times per week for a total fee of five dollars per barrel. The Saratoga was thrilled by my father's proposal because they were paying the city ten dollars per barrel with pickup once per week. It would save them five dollars per barrel, as well as free up valuable space in their kitchen. Most of all, frequent pickups would help eliminate the strong, smelly odor from their kitchen.

As a shrewd negotiator, my father had essentially created a "win-win" for the Saratoga Restaurant and for Coleman Crest. Daddy's *Cut the Crap and Close the Gap* strategy allowed us to eliminate the cost of feeding our hogs and generated a new revenue steam for our farm. Daddy's new agreement with the Saratoga allowed us to cut the crap and close the gap on our existing profitability gap between his desired and actual profitability.

Daddy told me that we would start picking up slop from the Saratoga Restaurant the next day. Instead of purchasing expensive corn from Southern States, we immediately began to pick up these big oil barrels of slop from the Saratoga Restaurant. When we arrived back at the farm after picking up our first load of slop from the Saratoga, our hogs started doing cartwheels as soon as our pickup entered the gate. They smelled the slop, and somehow they knew what was in store for them: a new menu that didn't include expensive corn from Southern States. Daddy and I drove the pickup through the field, and our hogs started to chase us. We stopped. I got up on the pickup bed and pushed over on the ground two fresh barrels of slop. Our hogs went wild.

After a couple of weeks of pouring out nearly twenty full barrels of fresh slop in their pen, the slop's strong odor made Coleman Crest the laughing stock in our small community. During my bus ride home from school with my friends, as we approached our farm, my friends began to make jokes about its terrible smell. I was completely embarrassed, but the severe gap between our desired versus our actual operating costs had been eliminated. After complaining to Daddy about my embarrassment, he quickly responded, "Don't worry about what your friends are laughing at. They will be laughing twenty-five years from now, and you will be gone away from here."

After six months of feeding our hogs a smelly, rich, high-cholesterol, sloppy mixture of prime rib, baked potato, and rotten vegetables, our hogs were about to burst. They had become so fat that they stopped breaking out; all they did was lay in their pens and sleep. They were so full from slop that they even stopped eating the slop I would pour onto the ground. It wasn't long before we began to establish a large inventory of leftover slop in our barn, and the flies and rats were having a Fourth of July reunion up in the barn! After telling Daddy about our backed-up inventory of slop, he summoned me to go up and down the road to ask our fellow farmer neighbors if they wanted to purchase our leftover slop for five dollars per barrel. I stopped by Cousin Liza's and Cousin Wills's first, and to my amazement, they agreed to purchase all of our leftover slop for our asking price of five dollars. They wanted to feed their hogs and make them fat just like ours.

Within nine months of launching our reengineered hog raising business model, Daddy and I had totally eliminated our Southern States corn costs and we were now generating a completely new revenue stream by picking up slop from the Saratoga Restaurant. Our hogs loved the slop more than they loved the corn, stopped breaking out and got fatter faster. Then, of course, we sold our excess slop to Cousin Liza and other fellow hog farmers, which allowed us to generate another five dollars per barrel. Now we were collecting five dollars from the Saratoga and generating an additional five dollars from selling our excess slop to neighboring farms for a total of ten dollars per barrel in new gross revenue.

Daddy's decision to cut the crap and close the gap in our desired cost versus our actual cost of our hog business would be a major reason why he was able to finance my college education five years later. Remaining in the hog business and reengineering it to make it more profitable is exactly what every CEO of every Fortune 500 company and small business attempts to do every day of the year to survive and to grow profits.

This is the first lesson in the *Cut the Crap and Close the Gap* management approach I received, and my teacher was my father. The lesson he taught me has formed the foundation for my long-term success, and I still rely on it every single day.

CLOSE THE GAP TAKEAWAYS:

- It's never too early to expect a child to think and behave like an adult—the sooner the better.
- Managing conflicting objectives is crucial to achieving desired results.
- There are always countless alternative, innovative options that we've never considered to transform our current level of performance.
- For starters, to achieve desired results, the option of quitting must be taken off the table.
- Every current business process offers opportunities for new revenue streams, new avenues for reducing costs, and new levels of productivity.

CHAPTER 4

HANG 'EM IN THE MIDDLE

Cut the Crap Principle 4: It's always better to
measure before we start our work than it is to
measure after we have performed our work.

Hang 'em in the middle" is what you do when you have to
make the best of a difficult, unfortunate situation. Every
Fourth of July, my family would have a family reunion.
Relatives from all over the country would return to Coleman
Crest to celebrate. The holiday was also my Uncle Ben's birthday,

so we always celebrated it, as well as my little cousin Stephen Wilson's birthday.

Two of our most important guests we looked forward to seeing were Uncle Stanford and Aunt Iva Dee. Uncle Stanford was highly respected by our entire family because he was a successful private practice physician in Dayton, Ohio. Uncle Stanford was very tall, smart and elegant. His wife, Aunt Iva Dee, was beautiful and very intelligent. Together, they represented success and royalty. When they arrived at the farm on Friday night before the big Saturday reunion, we rolled out the red carpet for them with a delicious country meal that included fried catfish, cornbread, brown beans, and fresh coleslaw. My parents would give up their bedroom and provide it to Uncle Stanford and Aunt Dee so they would feel totally comfortable and loved during their stay.

Cupcakes, Daddy and our whole family would work hard to prepare for our big family reunions. This meant that we needed to paint the walls inside our house, sand the floors, take the rugs to the cleaners, put the doorknobs back on the doors, and mow the fields of our farm.

In preparation for our big family reunion in 1974, Daddy wanted to spruce up our house by adding shutters to each of its windows. When Cupcakes and Daddy built our ranch-style home in 1950, they did everything to keep the cost to $10,000, which meant keeping unnecessary items like window shutters out of the budget. Daddy was a big believer in "we've got to satisfy needs first; then we'll get to satisfying wants later." He saw shutters as a want they could not afford. Twenty-four years later, Daddy decided to take the plunge and invest in new shutters for our big family reunion. He wanted to really impress Uncle Stanford with the improvements he had made to our house and the farm.

As a postal worker, Daddy had rotating days off from work, and he would dedicate this day to working with me on the farm. It was summer, and I always enjoyed Daddy taking the day off so we could work on a special farm project. Daddy was off on the Tuesday before the big Fourth of July family reunion on Saturday, and he planned to buy, paint, and hang shutters on each of our windows. When Daddy had told me a few days before about his plan, I literally could barely wait for Tuesday to come.

Daddy's strategic approach to project management was to "play it by ear." When he said, "We'll have to play it by ear," he meant, "Let's not make any concrete plans—instead, let's just see how things turn out, and then we will decide what to *do*." From the time Daddy lost his mother when he was a young child, to the time he was drafted to fight in World War II, to the time he had to juggle a job at the post office, manage our farm, be a waiter at private parties, be a deacon at the community church, and on top of all that, raise five children, "play it by ear" had become a necessary way of getting things done because nothing was ever certain or guaranteed. Daddy had found he always needed to be patient and flexible to survive and thrive.

I was always a little anxious about Daddy's play-it-by-ear strategy, especially when it came to managing a project. I had to always manage and restrain my excitement because I knew that Daddy's play-it-by-ear operating philosophy could enable him to change his plans.

This hot summer Tuesday before Saturday's big Fourth of July family reunion, Daddy and I started the day praying over our breakfast, a good, hot country meal, consisting of country bacon and sausage from our winter's hog slaughter, fried eggs, fried potatoes, grits, sourdough toast, a large glass of milk in a sterling silver cup, and a hot cup of coffee. As we ate, Daddy also fed scraps from the table to Butch, our little red dachshund. After breakfast, we watched *Town Talk*, a popular show that provided public service announcements about goings-on in Lexington.

After *Town Talk* and a brief nap, Daddy and I put Butch in our brown Chevrolet pickup truck, and we headed to Wick's, a local lumber company in Lexington. During our trip, Butch licked the dashboard uncontrollably like he always did, and Daddy began to smoke his Salem cigarettes. The pickup's cab was so full of smoke that I had to lower my window to breathe. We soon arrived at Wick's, smelling like smoke and Butch's vomit as a result of him licking the dashboard like crazy. Once we parked our pickup truck, Daddy, Butch, and I walked into the store to purchase the shutters.

Upon entering the store, Daddy's regular in-store salesman, Tommy, met us at the door. "Good afternoon, Mr. Coleman. How can I help you today?" he said. I really liked how my father was always greeted at Wick's, and I always loved hearing him say, "Put it on my bill," (without having to pay on the spot) at the end of any transaction he had with Wick's.

On this day, Daddy responded to Tommy, "We want to buy shutters for the house." Tommy said, "How many shutters do you want to buy, Mr. Coleman?" Daddy said, "Let me see here. We have six sets of windows on our home, so we will need twelve shutters." Tommy then said, "Okay, Mr. Coleman. What size do you need?" Daddy responded, "What size do you have?" Tommy then led Daddy, Butch, and me to a section with hundreds of shutters, starting with the small ones all the way up to the longer, larger shutters.

Daddy soon realized there was a large variety of shutter-size options, so he looked at the shutters in the middle of the inventory, pointed to them, and said, "We'll take twelve of those, the ones in the middle." Tommy then asked what paint color we wanted. "Green," Daddy said. After Tommy pulled twelve midsize shutters from the inventory and enough green paint for one coat on each shutter, along with brushes, Daddy, Butch, and I were ready to check out at the cashier's station. The cashier added everything up, and Daddy said, "Put it on my bill." The store attendant led us to our pickup to put everything on the truck, and off we were back to Coleman Crest.

Upon our arrival home, we took a break for lunch, but soon after, we started painting. And our work was nonstop. We had a lot of fun as we filled the time telling stories as we stroked the shutters with our brushes and played with Butch, trying to prevent him from rubbing up against the wet, green shutters.

Around 4:30 p.m. we finished painting all the shutters. Everything was green, including our hands, pants, and even Butch's red coat, which was now dark green. I gave Butch a good bath with turpentine and washed him down with our garden hose, and then he was red again. Daddy said, "We've worked up a storm. Let's go in the house and watch *The Rifleman*, take a break and have supper, and give these shutters a chance to dry.

Then we'll come back outside around six thirty, when the sky is still lit, and we'll start hanging our shutters on the house in time for Uncle Stanford's arrival this weekend."

After the *The Rifleman* and supper were over, I was really looking forward to hanging our shutters on the house. Daddy, Butch, and I went outside, and Daddy and I took the first pair of dry, freshly painted green shutters to the main front window. As Daddy held the hammer, along with a few nails, I placed the first shutter up against the window, and that's when we realized our big mistake. The shutters we had purchased were twenty-five inches long. Our windows were thirty-five inches long—ten inches longer than the shutters. After all our hard work and planning, and after we had already painted all of the shutters, I turned to Daddy and said, "Daddy, our shutters are too short. What are we going to do?" Daddy said, "We can't take 'em back to Wick's because we've already painted them, so let's hang 'em in the middle." And that's exactly what we did!

When Friday evening came around, Uncle Stanford and Aunt Dee pulled up into our driveway, and the first thing he mentioned was how nice the farm and the house looked. Not only did Uncle Stanford provide us with a good assessment, all of my other uncles and aunts and cousins were thoroughly impressed by the major improvements we had made to the farm and our house.

While Daddy, Butch and I could not close the gap in this case, Daddy had still applied the *Cut the Crap and Close the Gap* management approach by hanging the shutters in the middle instead of throwing them away and not having any shutters at all.

As the reader of this story, you may be asking yourself the following key question: why didn't you measure the windows before you left the farm for Wick's? The answer: we had to have breakfast, watch *Town Talk*, and take a break before going to town to purchase the shutters, so we just didn't have the time to measure the windows. You may also ask a follow-up question: why didn't you simply place one of the unpainted shutters up against the window before you started the painting process? The answer: we started painting after lunch and didn't have time to place the shutters up against the windows because we had to get the shutters all painted before *The Rifleman* and supper.

While it's hard to believe my answers provide valid excuses, in truth, they are similar to the common answers that employees in major corporations provide when they are planning the launch of a new product or service or the implementation of new information technology operating systems. It may be startling to the reader of this book to know that many economic and federal government studies have concluded that:

- Only 16.2 percent of software projects are completed on time and within budget (only 9 percent for big companies).
- 52.7 percent of IT projects will cost over 189 percent of their estimates.
- 31 percent of IT projects are canceled before they ever get completed.
- Companies and the federal government spend $81 billion a year on failed IT projects.

- 90 percent of new consumer products don't meet expectations.

Unfortunately, many companies and government agencies are unable to "hang 'em in the middle," and they simply take a multimillion dollar loss! The application of the *Cut the Crap and Close the Gap* management approach requires a combination of extensive collaboration, situational analysis, identification of the key issues, the development of tested strategies and tactics, and the development of a measurable action plan with key metrics and desired milestones.

All my young life, I heard our fellow neighbors say, "Measure twice. Cut once." On the day we had to hang the shutters, Daddy and I didn't make time to measure once before we cut. We were just too busy and preoccupied with other important priorities, like fixing and eating breakfast, watching *Town Talk*, preparing lunch, and making time for our favorite Western show, *The Rifleman*.

While it seems simple that all my father and I had to do was measure our windows before heading to Wick's, as managers, executives and business owners, we often become distracted with the pressures of limited time and competing priorities. Failing to allocate the time for effective strategic and project management can lead to missed opportunities and, at worst, failure and financial losses.

CLOSE THE GAP TAKEAWAYS:

- Quantifying the measurements and metrics of our desired results before we start our work can save us a lot of time, money, and frustration.
- We have to be careful not to become blinded by the enthusiasm of our desired results.
- Sometimes, competing priorities can distract us from effectively executing priorities that directly impact the attainment of our desired results.

CHAPTER 5

A MOTHER'S LETTER

Cut the Crap Principle 5: Second chances
are rare, but when they happen, aggressively
capitalize on them to achieve maximum success.

A Mother's Letter" is a story about how a little boy from a small family farm in Kentucky made it big, how a mother and a father provided a strong foundation for their son, and how the basic principles they taught him led to his tremendous success.

My mother was a saint who spoiled each of her five children and who supported my father in raising each of us. She was my rock star, my candle, and my searchlight. She never gave up on me, even when I had given up on myself.

We all have a story. My life story is titled "A Mother's Letter." It is about the purest form of unconditional love known to man: the love of his mother.

46

My mother was simply Cleo to her friends and her colleagues back home in Uttingertown, but as you know, I called her Cupcakes.

All my life, I tried to do everything possible to pass every test Cupcakes ever gave me and to make her happy. Most little boys grow up thinking their mothers are something special. They think their mothers are the prettiest, most loving, and most precious beings on the planet. To me, Cupcakes really was.

My father, Sam, was an amazing and powerful man, but Cupcakes was my first love, my first teacher, and my first friend. Cupcakes was my fan club. Throughout her life, she shared and cared and laughed and cried with her family and friends. She was a social worker, a true Southern belle, a Lady Kentuckian at heart, and she was a faithful Christian.

Cupcakes faced and tackled all the giants in her life. Each and every day she lived, she refused to be a victim to her giants. She fought all sorts of giants, including poverty as a young child, racism, and the loss of her dear mother one day after she graduated from college. She had a demanding career and made tremendous sacrifice to send all five of her children to college. She returned to college to obtain a master's degree at age forty-five and fought valiantly against terrible illnesses, including breast, colon, and finally lung cancer, until she died at age seventy-three in 2012.

Cupcakes instilled confidence in me to take on my own giants. She had a calm way of challenging me to learn and grow. At age seven, I remember Cupcakes telling me I was going to be like those Kennedy boys (John, Bobby, and Edward Kennedy) because I had used the word "personification" to explain why my Dalmatian could talk. When my Cupcakes told me this, I believed I could become President of the United States if I was willing to campaign for the position.

Cupcakes always encouraged me to perform well in school. She would work with me on my homework late into the evenings. I loved how she would spend long hours with me at the kitchen table after supper to help me complete a book report or an essay.

After I would finish my homework each evening, we would go outside and sit on our front porch. I would fix Cupcakes a cold Falls City Beer in her favorite frosted mug with a salted head and bring out a plate of her favorite cold cuts, pickles, cheese, and Ritz Crackers. I loved serving Cupcakes her favorite appetizers. She loved it, and so did I. She would always say, "Ah, baby, this is just what Momma needs."

I remember on hot summer nights when the dark sky was lit up by thousands of stars and lightening bugs were flying in the air. I would stand at the edge of the porch, look out into the field in front of our house, and I would make a speech as if I were a preacher or a politician. Cupcakes would listen to my speeches as if I were Dr. Martin Luther King or Rev. Taylor, our pastor at the Uttingertown Baptist Church. Cupcakes would correct my grammar and would encourage me to speak louder, with more passion and clarity. I loved her coaching and encouragement. She made me feel like important and her encouragement and coaching had a positive impact on my confidence in speaking to audiences at church and at school.

As the years progressed, my relationship with Cupcakes grew even closer. I could barely wait until early Saturday morning when my father would leave for work; then I'd run into her bedroom and give her a big hug while she was still in the bed. She would tell me to reach for the letter that my father would leave her on the dresser in their bedroom, which provided details of our chores for the day. Cupcakes would ask me to read my father's letter, and when I was finished, she'd say, "He's crazy, but I guess we better get up and get our work done before that crazy man gets back home!"

My first lesson in setting priorities and organizing the work that needed to be completed was provided by helping Cupcakes manage and complete my father's list of chores. Even with all the chores we had to complete, I would still talk to my mother all day long about our family's history as well as political, financial, health, and religious issues and many other topics.

Cupcakes was a master strategist and multitasker. She had a full-time job as a social worker at Eastern State Hospital and was a full-time mother and a full-time wife. She used to always say, "I need to go to work to get a break!" She accomplished so much with limited resources and limited time. After work, she would take my sister Rhetta to tap and ballet practice and then pick me up from marching band practice. During our summer breaks from school, I would call her at work just to hear her voice and to talk with her awhile. She made it clear to her staff that when I called, they needed to announce over the intercom that she had a call from me, no matter what she was doing. Her assistant, Mrs. Margaret Wolfe, was so nice and supportive, and I greatly appreciated her help in dispatching my mother to the phone. My mother used to say, "Y'all think I own this place (Eastern State Hospital)." And she was right. I did think she owned Eastern State Hospital and I always felt like I was her most important priority.

I attended Brian Station High School, a combination city/country school where I played second trumpet in a highly competitive and accomplished band that won the state championship my sophomore year. I focused on academics and graduated with a solid B average, even though I worked the family farm year-round, with full-time responsibility during summers for raising cows, hogs, chickens, corn, and tobacco.

In 1977, I began searching for a college to attend. Cupcakes always wanted me to attend Howard University. Many of her heroes had gone there, including Patricia Harris, Vernon Jordan, and Thurgood Marshall. Cupcakes wanted me to receive a first-class education like those Kennedy boys. "They may have gone to Harvard, but you are going to Howard," she would say. I think she had the same plans and dreams for me as Rose Kennedy had for her sons.

Cupcakes helped me complete and submit my application to Howard, and I anxiously waited to hear Howard's decision about my acceptance. A few months after I submitted my application to Howard, my family and I returned from a family trip to Cincinnati. I reached into our mailbox on the road in front of our farm, and I found a letter from Howard's Admissions Department. I ran back to the car and began to read the letter to my mother. I frowned. My request for admission to Howard had been denied.

Cupcakes was furious about Howard's decision, and she refused to concede to it. She could not accept how this could happen to her future Martin Luther King Jr., her John Kennedy.

She said, "Baby, don't worry. I'm going to write a letter to the president of Howard to get them to change their decision." I said, "Momma, come on. What is that going to do? They don't know you, and they don't care."

She continued, "Baby, trust in me and trust in the Lord, and we will fix this problem, and you will be going to Howard in the fall." I saw my mother write her letter late into the evening. After completing her letter, she put it in an envelope that was addressed to Howard's president, Dr. James E. Cheek. Before I went to bed, she asked me to put her sealed envelope that enclosed her letter, into our mailbox the following morning.

Cupcakes later told me that she wrote, "Dr. Cheek, please give my son a second chance. He may not be the smartest little boy, but you will find that he is the hardest working boy who ever attended Howard. If you let him attend and graduate from Howard, he will be a great man, and he will give back to Howard in many ways. Please put him on probation for the first semester, if you have to, but please give my son a second chance."

Cupcakes told me to never tell anyone until after she was gone that she had to write her letter on my behalf because she didn't want my brothers and sisters to think she was playing favorites, and she also didn't want Mrs. Perkins, the Howards, a prominent family in our community and the rest of our neighbors to think I was slow.

Even though Cupcakes sent her letter, I gave up on my dreams of attending Howard, and I began to prepare to attend Kentucky State, my parents' alma mater. But my mother never gave up on my dreams to go to Howard, and she never gave up on me.

About two months after Cupcakes sent her letter to Howard's president, I received another letter in the mail from Howard's Admissions Department. This new letter explained that their earlier decision to decline my request for admission had been reversed and that I was now approved to attend Howard on a probationary basis.

On my first day at the university, when I arrived at Sutton Plaza, an off-campus dorm on Fourteenth Street in Washington, DC, I met Rushern Baker, who would become one of my dearest friends. Rushern had a New England accent, and I later told my mother that I'd met this smart guy who sounded like he was from London. During that first evening, Rushern and a few of my other friends, Richard Chaney and David Byrd and I walked throughout Washington. As we passed the front of the White House, Rushern expressed a great deal of respect for the presidency and a strong desire to serve the public in an elected position.

Rushern was with me when I met the prettiest girl who attended Howard. He and I were taking a study break in Howard's Founder's Library. Suddenly, this sophisticated, beautiful young lady walked in front of our desk. I looked up and said, "Rushern, look at that babe in that beautiful dress. Who is that?" Rushern said, "I know. Her name is Cathy Clash, and she is beautiful. She's in my Latin course, and she's the only one passing the class." I said, "Rushern, she is going to be my wife someday!" Rushern replied, "Right, she wouldn't have either one of us!"

A few months later, when I was managing Rushern's campaign for sophomore class president in liberal arts, we saw Cathy Clash walking across campus. We ran toward her so we could introduce ourselves to her. I said, "My name is James Coleman. Rushern Baker is running for class president of the sophomore class in liberal arts. Can we get your support?" Cathy told us she could not vote for Rushern because she was in the engineering school. I told her that was okay and we needed everybody's help. I then asked her for her phone number, and she gave it. A day later, I called Cathy to invite her to lunch to tell her more about our campaign. When I called her, she was cleaning her room. I invited her to the Howard Inn, and I'll always remember that she ordered a tuna melt for lunch.

Rushern's and my public service career started when we were at Howard. Rushern was elected president of the sophomore class in liberal arts, which provided him with the experience and credibility to later be elected to become president of the Liberal Arts Student Council. During his campaign for student council president, Rushern asked me to be his campaign manager. I was thrilled and accepted the position. I built our team of volunteers, as well as helped Rushern attend all his campaign appearances. As his campaign manager, I used all the skills I had learned from managing Coleman Crest Farm in Kentucky. The one skill I especially employed was "being resourceful"—this was one of the most important management skills my father had taught me. My father could see value where others couldn't.

While at Howard, I met many other brilliant young people who had goals of becoming doctors, lawyers, business leaders, and politicians. Many of the students had famous parents and were from big cities like Chicago and New York, but we were all in the same boat now. I remember meeting Sanita Jackson (Jesse Jackson's daughter) for the first time. We were among other fellow students, and we all began to tell each other our names, where we were from, as well as our parents' names. Sanita said, "I'm Sanita Jackson from Chicago, and my father's name is Jesse." I said, "Nice to meet you, Sanita. I'm James Coleman from Lexington, Kentucky, and my father's name is Sam!"

My first choice for a major was chemistry because I wanted to be a successful and wealthy physician like my Uncle Stanford. Uncle Stanford and his wife, Aunt Dee, resided in a beautiful new home that had two floors, a garage with an electric door, a basement that did not leak, and hopscotch painted on the basement floor. I felt that whatever job Uncle Stanford had, I wanted to do the same because I wanted to have a beautiful home just like he had.

While I was committed to studying chemistry in preparation for entrance into medical school, I learned that chemistry was not the right fit for me. I called my mother to tell her the news that I had decided to change my major and hoped she and my father wouldn't be disappointed by it. My mother told me that I would make a good businessman like her father and my grandfather, and she encouraged me to change my major to economics, and I did. I enjoyed the subject because it gave me a chance to debate with fellow students and learn more about our nation's economy.

As a result of Cupcakes's letter on my behalf to Dr. Cheek, I was blessed to enjoy a college experience that allowed me to grow, learn and be exposed to unlimited possibilities and many brilliant people who have become my best friends and Cathy Clash who graduated with honors from Howard's School of Engineering as a Chemical Engineer and later became my wife after we graduated from Howard. I became the president of the liberal arts student council and was selected by Dr. James Cheek to be in the *Who's Who Among Students in American Universities and Colleges*. This all happened because Cupcakes believed in me. Most of all, Cupcakes took the time to write her letter to Dr. Cheek that absolutely changed my life forever.

As a result of my mother's love and determination to get me enrolled and to graduate from Howard University, I've enjoyed a wonderful sales and marketing career that has enabled me to work and live in thirteen cities across the United States.

Cupcakes applied the *Cut the Crap and Close the Gap* management approach by changing the perception of me as a prospective student not up to the challenge of Howard to convincing Dr. Cheek that I was worth the risk of being admitted to the university. My mother's letter gave me a chance to learn from many of Americas most dynamic professors and to become a model alum of this great, prestigious university that I now call my alma mater, Howard University.

CLOSE THE GAP TAKEAWAYS:

- Life can take you from being a college reject to being a Who's Who Among Students in American Universities and Colleges inductee—if you just don't give up.
- Don't accept no so fast. Just know that someone else has experienced the same kind of setback, and they

succeeded because they didn't give up or accept no for an answer.

- Converting a no into a yes is always negotiable, but don't wait on the person who said no to start the negotiation.
- A mother's unconditional love is the most precious and powerful love anyone can ever experience.

CHAPTER 6

A BAMA HAS ARRIVED

Cut the Crap Principle 6: Don't judge a person by what
they wear, how they talk or where they were born.
Everybody has disabilities, and everybody has abilities.

T he night before Cupcakes, Bubba, Coley, and my sister
Rhetta drove me from Lexington Kentucky to Washington,
DC, to attend Howard University, Daddy summoned
me to his master bedroom. He was sitting in his tan-brown
leather La-Z-Boy chair, looking like the Godfather with his

stern, careful, and deliberate facial expressions. He started our conversation by telling me to reach into his drawer for a large envelope with the words "Citizen's Union Bank" written on it. I did as he instructed, and Daddy said, "Take a look at the check inside of the envelope." I did and found a certified cashier's check for my first year of tuition at Howard.

Daddy said, "Take this check to the administration building where you have to pay your tuition bills, and they will take care of it." He went on to explain, "I told you that if you would help me on the farm over the last few years, I would send you to college, and I am going to send you to Howard, and I am going to pay for all of it. Some of it will come from the proceeds from the farm, but I also had to take out a large loan on the farm that you will probably have to pay-off after I'm dead and gone."

I couldn't believe it. I held the ticket for what seemed to be my seat on the "Underground Railroad," and Daddy had delivered on his promise just like he said he would. Daddy said, "I'm not going to be able to drive to Washington with you tomorrow morning with your mother and brothers and sister because I have to go to work, but do well in school. I will be praying for you." After that, Daddy hugged me, sending me off to freedom and my journey to a whole new world.

After I arrived for my first semester at Howard in 1978, I walked to the administration building on a very hot August day to pay for my tuition, only to find many of my classmates angrily standing outside in front of the administration building in a long line. They were from big, fancy cities like New York, Detroit, Chicago, and Los Angles, places I dreamed of visiting. They all seemed to be well groomed and neatly dressed in the latest fashions. Compared to these students, I looked like Forrest Gump, a country bumpkin. One of the coolest guys in line yelled out to everyone and introduced me as "The Bama from Kentucky" because I was wearing a red and white checkered plaid shirt with a pair of fresh blue jeans. My mother had purchased them for me for school.

The sun was blistering, and I grew more and more frustrated as I stood in line. There had to be a better way of paying my tuition other than standing in that long line while being called a "Bama" and becoming embarrassed in front of all those beautiful, young Howard female students.

So instead of staying in that line of more than 200 students, I did what Daddy would have done—I stepped out of line, walked up to the door, introduced myself to somebody with authority, and asked if there were options other than wasting a lot of time standing in line in the heat.

When I stepped out of line, the other students had a field day. They wondered aloud what this "Bama from Kentucky" was thinking. Not only was I considered a so-called Bama, I was also considered a stupid Bama for giving up my coveted space in line.

As I approached the administration building's steps, I spotted a security officer who seemed to have a lot of authority. The officer approached me and said I would have to return all the way to the back of the line to pay my tuition bill, no ifs, ands, or buts. Before accepting his marching orders, I asked him why the line was so long. He said all of the students were waiting on their grants and scholarships to be processed, a monumental task the administrative staff had to manually perform. I told the officer that I was not waiting on a grant and certainly not a scholarship, and he quipped, assuming that all of the students were dependent on grants and scholarships, "If you don't have a grant or a scholarship, you might as well head to the Greyhound bus station because you won't be going to Howard University." At that point, I reached in my pocket and handed him the envelope that Daddy had given to me the night before I left Kentucky for Howard.

The officer looked at my multicolored check and said, "This is a certified check. It's as good as cash, and you can go on into the administration building and up to the window at Student Accounts to submit the check." So I walked into the administration building and encountered only three students in line who were also paying with a certified check.

Here I was, a so-called Bama from Kentucky, paying my tuition with a certified check produced from the sale of slop and hogs and a loan taken out on Coleman Crest, and I was now standing in the short line. That day, I learned that hard work and cutting the crap and closing the gap can improve our quality of life. I also learned that having money doesn't always solve our problems, but it can certainly enable us to stand in the "short line of life," even if the people we pass by in line are laughing at us for having the courage to challenge conventional wisdom.

When I returned back to my dorm later in the evening, all of my classmates were amazed that I'd paid for all of my classes. Most of them said that their parents did not have the financial resources to pay for their college tuition and that they were relying on grants and scholarships to attend school. I was so moved by the feeling of being truly blessed that I called my parents collect around 9 p.m. I remember it like it was yesterday when the operator said, "I have a collect call coming in from James Coleman, do you accept?" and Cupcakes replied, "Yes, is everything all right?" And even before I answered her, I simply said, "Hello, Cupcakes I have something to tell you and Daddy, is Daddy there?" And she said, "Yes." She rushed to wake him up to get him on the other phone so the three of us were connected. Then I heard Daddy say, "Is everything alright?" They were conditioned to hearing abrupt bad news. I said, "Momma and Daddy, I just want to say thank you for your hard work and sacrifice for sending me to Howard and for paying for my college tuition instead of having me to wait in long lines for grants and scholarships." Daddy replied again, "Is everything alright?" I said, "Yes, Daddy. Everything is alright, and I love you and Momma very much," and that was the end of our short call. Cupcakes later told me that Daddy had said after the call, "That boy's lost his mind. What's wrong with him?" He'd thought it was odd for me to call him to thank him for something he felt was his sole responsibility—paying for my college education.

The next five years were an incredible learning experience for me. I was fortunate to have two sets of cousins who lived in Prince George's County, a beautiful suburb outside of Washington, DC. They took care of me on the weekends, helped me end my homesickness, and assured me I would graduate from Howard one day and make my family proud. I'll never forget the generosity of my dear cousin Dr. Stanford Coleman Jr. and his wife, Paula, and my other dear cousins,

Trish and Harvey Hankins, for their unconditional love and support. I learned that no matter where I traveled, my parents would pray for me on their knees every night, asking the Lord to send guardian angels to protect me every day of my life.

CLOSE THE GAP TAKEAWAYS:

- Daddy always used to tell me, "Don't worry about people laughing at you. They will be laughing twenty years from now when you are a success."
- Money doesn't always solve our problems. Money is just a tool that helps us to better cope and respond to our problems.
- No currency replaces the access to cold cash.
- Hard work and sacrifice always pays off in the end.
- Be careful in your judgment of others until you have really gained insight into their journey.

CHAPTER 7

OH, I WISH I WERE AN OSCAR MAYER MANAGER

Cut the Crap Principle 7: Always provide the most
positive answer with the least amount of words.
Countless deals have been lost from talking too much.

n December 1982, my oldest sister and cherished mentor, Ruth, paid for me to travel to San Francisco to spend time with her during the holidays. I couldn't believe that I made the long trip across the country. When I stepped off the plane, I hugged Ruth and said, "I made it. I can do this." Ruth was and still to this day is a "trailblazer," unafraid to travel anywhere and willing to take on any challenge. Ruth was the first woman and the first African-American to graduate from the University of Kentucky's Civil Engineering Department with a bachelor's degree in civil engineering. She later secured her professional engineering (PE) license, and then she secured a big job as a civil engineer at the world's largest civil engineering company, Bechtel Corporation, headquartered in San Francisco.

During my Christmas vacation, Ruth promised we would fly to Los Angeles to see her good friends Joe and Francis Smith. Joe and Francis were a beautiful couple she'd met while attending Transylvania University in Lexington. Ruth wanted me to learn from Joe how to get a good job in sales with IBM after graduating Howard in May of 1983. I was quite impressed with Joe. He had a beautiful wife; a brand-new, beautiful home in Thousand Oaks, California; a brand-new Porsche in the garage; and a swimming pool in the back yard. He was a young executive with IBM, the hottest technology company on the planet at the time.

Joe and Francis looked and acted like they were wealthy movie stars, and to me they really were. Joe advised me on how to prepare for my interview at Howard's placement office with IBM. He said it would be a good idea to interview with at least five to ten other companies first before interviewing with IBM because IBM was a tough company to get into. Joe also told me to use the "needs/satisfaction" approach with the interviewer at the placement office. This meant staying focused on the interviewer's and the company's needs and showing them how I could satisfy those needs. I was very impressed with Joe and his advice, and I could barely wait to get back to Howard in January to sign up for several interviews with many of America's top Fortune 500 companies. I was ready to interview for a career in sales.

Upon my return to Washington after my wonderful vacation with Ruth, I stopped by the Howard University placement office. I signed up to interview with Oscar Mayer & Company and a few other well-known big-brand companies. I did everything I could think of to prepare for my interview with Oscar Mayer; however, it was all practice because I was aiming to get a good sales job at IBM so I could strike it rich, just like Joe, and capture the American Dream, with a beautiful wife, kids, a big house, swimming pool, a fast sports car, and plenty of money to burn!

I remember like it was yesterday when I was called from the waiting room inside the placement office to enter a small office to be interviewed by Jeffery Parker, a corporate recruiter for Oscar Mayer. Mr. Parker was a handsome, well-groomed corporate executive who'd grown up in Alabama. He was a Southern gentleman. He did his best to make me comfortable by asking a few nice, easy questions. He started with, "Howard has a great football team, don't they?" I said yes. Then he went on to say, "Howard's got a good track team too, don't they?"

At this point, I felt I needed to take control of the interview and use everything Joe had taught me over the holidays. I responded by saying, "Mr. Parker, I'm here to make a difference at Oscar Mayer & Company. I'm here to interview for a career with Oscar Mayer if you are prepared to have that discussion with me." I had nothing to lose because my sights were set on IBM. Mr. Parker couldn't believe how assertive and confident I was behaving in the interview in response to his polite icebreaker questions. He then had me discuss why I felt I would be a good candidate for employment at Oscar Mayer. Thirty minutes later, he cut me off right in the middle of answering his questions and said, "What's your grade point average?" Kind of startled by the question, I quickly responded 3.0, which is exactly what I had received the fall semester of 1982. However, my cumulative grade point average was 2.4, a result of being on probation earlier in my first year when I'd struggled with organic chemistry and engineering calculus in my fruitless efforts to become a chemist and later a medical doctor. If I'd told Mr. Parker that my grade point average was 2.4, the interview would have been over because they were looking for at least a 3.0 and higher. Mr. Parker wrote down "3.0," then looked me in the eye and said, "Look, you have done a great job in the interview, and I would like to do something that is very different. I would like to invite you to Madison, Wisconsin, to interview with our senior management team for a positon in our Pre-Management Training Program (PMTP)."

The PMTP was usually reserved for students with a concentration in brand marketing, materials management, and finance who had received MBAs from prestigious universities. Mr. Parker told me his executive assistant would contact me to confirm the date I'd fly to Madison to visit the Oscar Mayer headquarters for my big interview. And that was the end of my first interview.

I went to the nearest pay phone and told Ruth about my successful interview with Oscar Mayer. While I was excited, I was scared that I had made a big mistake. I admitted to Ruth that I'd told Mr. Parker my grade point average was a 3.0, which was the truth since he did not ask whether it was for the past semester or a cumulative grade point average. Ruth calmed my nerves and said, "Don't worry; everything is going to be fine. Just explain it when you get there if it even comes up, and it probably won't." Ruth's comfort and support calmed me immediately.

The following week, Mr. Parker's secretary called me and explained all my travel arrangements and told me about the nice hotel, the Black Hawk Hotel, which they had booked for me. I was excited until she said at the end of our call, "Oh, by the way, please bring an original copy of your college transcripts with you for our files." I said with confidence, "I sure will," but deep inside I felt that my opportunity with Oscar Mayer had just evaporated right before my eyes, even before my plane had a chance to take off for Madison. My heart was racing after that scary call with Mr. Parker's secretary, and immediately I called Ruth again. As always, she calmed me down. She said, "If Oscar Mayer makes hiring decisions strictly on a candidate's grades, they won't be in business for long, and besides, you will be working for IBM when you graduate in May anyway."

On a cold January day, my plane took off from Washington National Airport to Chicago O'Hare for a changeover flight to Madison, Wisconsin. During the entire flight, I felt so blessed to have parents who had sacrificed so much for me to be on this plane. I studied all the materials that Mr. Parker's secretary had sent me, including Oscar Mayer's annual report, an informational pamphlet about Oscar Mayer's Pre-Management Training Program, and other newspaper articles and memos about the company. Once I landed at O'Hare, I thought I had landed in another country in that big ol' airport. I was so impressed, seeing all the important and busy business travelers running fast to catch their flights as I walked through the terminal to catch the last flight of my trip to Madison on a small carrier called Ozark Airlines.

Once I found my seat on the Ozark jet, I was sitting next to a gentleman who seemed like a very serious business executive. Immediately, I reached for my Oscar Mayer materials to take another opportunity to prepare for my interviews. Once we were wheels up and into our flight, the businessman asked if I worked for Oscar Mayer. No, I told him, but added that I was heading to Madison for an interview with the company. He introduced himself as Tom Smith and said he worked for Oscar Mayer. Mr. Smith told me I would like working for the company if I got the opportunity, and he wished me the best in my interview. I thanked Mr. Smith for his kind feedback about Oscar Mayer and his positive encouragement for my upcoming interview. I then went back to reading my Oscar Mayer materials with a focus on being totally prepared for the upcoming interview. An hour later, we were landing in

Madison, and Mr. Smith again wished me good luck as we got off the plane.

As Mr. Smith and I walked to the baggage claim area, his wife and kids were running to greet and hug him, making it seem like he had been overseas traveling for years. Mr. Smith introduced me to his family and then asked where the company was putting me up. I told him that I was booked for the Black Hawk Hotel, and Mr. Smith said, "Oh, that's a nice hotel. We'll give you a ride in our car there." And off we went to Mr. Smith's family station wagon that was parked in the airport's parking lot. When we got into his car, the engine wouldn't start because the battery had frozen due to below-zero temperatures outside. Mr. Smith called a tow truck, and in minutes a driver arrived to give his battery a warm charge. Then the car started, and we headed to the Black Hawk.

After arriving at the Black Hawk Hotel, the Smiths let me out of their car, and Mr. Smith shook my hand firmly and, again, wished me good luck in my interviews. All I knew about Mr. Smith was that he was a very nice gentleman and a great representative for Oscar Mayer. After saying goodbye to the Smiths, I checked into the hotel and went to sleep with a full head of knowledge about Oscar Mayer and an original transcript that showed a cumulative grand point average of 2.4.

It was the following morning, and after a good, long sleep at the Black Hawk Hotel, now it was time for me to perform. I was nervous *and* confident. When I finally arrived at the lobby of Oscar Mayer's headquarters, I fell in love with the building's smell. It reminded me of the sweet smell of bacon and country ham back home in Kentucky. Mr. Parker's secretary came out and escorted me to meet with him in his office. Mr. Parker stood up from his chair and shook my hand to welcome me to Madison and to Oscar Mayer & Company.

As a real Southern gentleman would do, Mr. Parker asked about my flight and if I enjoyed staying at the Black Hawk. I had nothing but good news about all the wonderful arrangements he and his secretary had prepared for my trip. Mr. Parker then started to explain my action-packed interview schedule for the day. He began mentioning the names of all the top executives I would meet. When he got to the name Tom Smith, I stopped him to say that I met a man on the plane last night who said his name was Tom Smith and that he worked for Oscar Mayer. Mr. Parker was shocked by the coincidence and said, "You met Tom Smith?" I described Mr. Smith's appearance. My description fit the man that Mr. Parker knew. Immediately, he informed me that Tom Smith was the company's vice president of brand marketing and would be instrumental in deciding whether I'd become employed at Oscar Mayer. Mr. Parker was happy to hear that I had a great time on the flight with Mr. Smith, and he was also excited to hear that the Smiths drove me to the hotel from the airport.

Later on in this preparatory meeting, Mr. Parker asked the big question that I was hoping would never be asked: "Did you bring an original copy of your transcript?" I said yes and handed him the transcript . . . and all hell broke loose for a short time. Mr. Parker looked at my transcript, and he immediately looked back at me, biting his teeth. "I thought you said you had a 3.0. Your transcript says 2.4." Immediately, I explained that during the interview, I thought he was asking about the previous fall semester in which I did receive at 3.0 grade point average, and that I didn't know he asking about my cumulative grade point average.

At this time, I knew there were only two options left: Mr. Parker would send me packing to the airport, never to return to Madison, or he would just give it a try to see if I could get through the day without grades becoming an issue. Fortunately, Mr. Parker chose the latter option, and the second best day in my life, only second to the day I was accepted to Howard University, was just about to begin. Mr. Parker said, "Look, it's on you. I can't believe you did this. I'm going to put your resume at the bottom of these papers in your file that you will provide to each interviewer at the beginning of the interview, and if grades come up, it's all on you to explain this mess!" This was not the time for me to "play it by ear" as my father had explained to me more than ten years earlier when I was a little boy. I promised Mr. Parker that I would do a good job in the interviews, and I apologized for the misunderstanding.

My first big interview of the day was with Mr. Tom Duesler, a short, slightly overweight, mean-looking man who was the group vice president of sales and marketing. As Mr. Parker walked me into Mr. Duesler's office for the interview, Mr. Duesler stared at me intently while I sat down; then he demanded Mr. Parker leave his office. After Mr. Parker left, Mr. Duesler pushed my file to the side, refusing to even open the folder and look at my resume, application, and my official college transcript, and he began to tear into me. "I don't care where you went to school, and I don't care how well you did in school. Everybody here in this place went to a good school, and everybody's got good grades like you have. I want you to tell me right now why you want to work at Oscar Mayer." Immediately, I said, "Oh, I wish I were an Oscar Mayer manager. This is what I truly wish I could be, 'cause if I were an Oscar Mayer manager, all my life would be happy and free!" Mr. Duesler said, "I love it. That was great!"

I then started to tell him my life story of growing up on a hog farm that was purchased by my great-grandfather in 1888, working hard, doing as I was told under a tough dad, cutting hogs and slaughtering them in the fall, bailing hay, and raising tobacco. Mr. Duesler was seduced. By the time Mr. Parker came in to end the interview, my interview with Mr. Duesler had already gone forty minutes beyond the planned time. Mr. Parker could not believe how I had tamed this corporate lion. I stood up and shook Mr. Duesler's hand, and he wished me good luck.

As I was leaving Mr. Duesler's office, Mr. Tom Smith, who had given me a ride with his family in his station wagon from the Madison airport to the Black Hawk Hotel just the evening before, was now waiting at the door outside of Mr. Duesler's office, and he said to me, "Hello, Jim, how did it go with Tom?" Mr. Parker was very impressed at how Mr. Smith admired me and encouraged me. It was as if Mr. Smith had already become my mentor, and it lifted Mr. Parker's confidence in me for what I would face in other interviews throughout the rest of the day with other executives. The rest of my day went very well, meeting with at least seven of Oscar Mayer's senior-level executives. By the end of it, I met with Mr. Parker in his office to discuss the feedback he had received from my executive interviewers. He asked me about the day. I told him that I loved every part of it. Mr. Parker then laid it on me. "We want to hire you for our Pre-Management Training Program at $23,000 per year. Do you have any questions?" I said, "Yes, I accept your offer, and can I call my mother to tell her the good news?" He stood up, gleaming at me, hugged me, and left the room so I could call my mother with the good news while she was at work. When Mrs. Wolfe, my mother's executive assistant, connected me to her, I told Cupcakes I'd just been hired by Oscar Mayer at $23,000 a year plus healthcare benefits, and she began to cry with excitement on the phone. It was truly one of the best days of my life, and it still is today.

In May 1983, I was an official employee of Oscar Mayer & Company and the only non-MBA ever to be hired into the PMTP program. This program was intended to be a learning experience, allowing for close-working relationships with multiple functional areas critical to understanding Oscar Mayer's business. Following an intense, seven-month training period, I "graduated" and was assigned the tough New York City territory as a sales representative for Oscar Mayer meats, Claussen Pickles, and Chef's Pantry prepared foods. I was responsible for three retail chains serviced by Royal Foods Distributors, with annual sales of $2 million. The diverse environment of Spanish Harlem and surrounding areas did not hamper my ability to build the business. I quickly learned to speak Spanish and Arabic and picked up key communications skills to earn my customers' respect. I learned to love the hustle and bustle of up-and-down-the-street sales, helping to grow my customers' businesses and earning the "Oscar Mayer Sales Council Ring" my first year.

In May 1985, I was promoted to account supervisor and moved to Washington, DC. I was responsible for managing twelve military commissaries, accounting for $3 million in sales, and representing more than 30 percent of the Washington, DC, market. In a highly price-driven environment, I motivated my merchandisers through a variety of contests and organized product demonstrations to increase product interest. My sales volume increased 8 percent by the end of my first year.

By the end of 1985, I was heavily recruited to join Pepsi USA in their fountain beverage division and decided that the opportunity offered the career challenge I desired. Pepsi had just started the Pepsi USA Fountain Beverage Division, and they were looking for talent to jumpstart their endeavor. As the Philadelphia franchise manager, I was a combination bottler consultant and national account manager. I had direct responsibility for the development of the on-premises business for the franchise and corporate-operated bottling operations within the Delaware Valley.

As a Pepsi USA franchise manager, I was accountable for delivering fountain volume objectives, new outlet distribution, and indirect management of the bottler's sales organization with total sales of $8.5 million. I set a goal of achieving a 15 percent profit increase through a combination of new business and cost-cutting strategies. I successfully developed and launched a strategy to change Coca-Cola fountain accounts to Pepsi. I coordinated and launched the "Penetrate the Penetrated" blitz where I led the local bottlers to sell additional Pepsi brands to their existing fountain accounts. I successfully sold in the Orange Slice and the Lemon Lime Slice line at a multi-store Burger King and Wendy franchisee, which rapidly grew overall fountain sales and enabled me to achieve my 15 percent profit increase objective.

In April 1989, I was promoted to retail sales operations manager with responsibility for retail sales, distribution, and profit and loss. I managed four sales managers and forty-one account managers, as well as the in-store relationships with Pathmark, Super Fresh, Acme, Clemens, and Thriftway accounts, representing $40 million in sales across 226 stores in the Philadelphia/Delaware Valley market. This was a combination of managing people and operations and having responsibility for eighteen bulk delivery trucks and customer service representatives. I hired, trained, and motivated my people, promoting two to district managers, and I delivered a 4 percent growth rate in eight short months.

In January 1990, I moved to Pepsi's New York headquarters as associate retail sales training manager. As a new training manager, I was certified as an instructor for Development Dimensions International performance and interaction management training program. I developed and conducted sales and management training programs for entry-level retail sales representatives and district managers nationally. I facilitated performance management and selling skills training programs throughout the country, projecting a highly motivating facilitation style. I also made a solid contribution to the training department by developing a "Transferred Learning Evaluation" program to analyze the impact of the various training programs and to select opportunities for continuous improvement.

As an associated retail sales training manger, I enjoyed the opportunity to travel to every major market in the United States. Furthermore, this position enabled me to enhance my motivational speaking capabilities that led to my long-term success in future executive positions.

I had been promised a region manager position in either the retail or fountain sales organizations. Shortly after, Pepsi USA and Pepsi Bottling Group merged, and that promise became a reality. In August 1991, I moved to Kalamazoo, Michigan, as a region manager responsible for five account managers and thirteen customer service representatives. I reported to the area vice president and quickly became involved in the development of the on-premises channel for businesses in the Southern Michigan markets, including the Meijer Convenience Stores, Michigan Pizza Hut, Stanton Wendy's Inc., P/S Foodmarts, and Michigan State University accounts. Along with training my staff on sales and management skills, I achieved the following:

- Developed a promotional plan for P/S Foodmarts that created excitement, increased revenues, and grew sales 5 percent through a 32-oz. and 44-oz. "Glow Bottle" program, and increased radio advertising funded by the incremental dollars.
- Instituted a "Zero S&D" program at Pizza Hut whereby they could buy the larger size plastic cups and syrup from Pepsi, thus consolidating their resource needs.

This sale increased syrup revenues and supply income, and, in turn, paid for my region's S&D expenses.

- Renewed Michigan State University's contract, despite Coca-Cola's aggressive competitive effort. I achieved this tremendous success by creatively funding a large scholarship program, establishing quarterly promotional program initiatives, and increasing campus vending.

In December 1992, I was promoted to business development manager, a field-trade marketing assignment, in the Cleveland, Ohio, market. I was responsible for developing the noncommercial channel of business in Ohio, Indiana, Missouri, and Illinois, with such major accounts as TWA, Service America, Canteen, ARA, Baxter Healthcare, and all major universities, totaling $50 million in retail sales.

To generate improved awareness about the noncommercial business sector, I instituted an advisory council within the five business units to help develop and exchange ideas on how to grow volume in the schools, hospitals, and airlines. I led and facilitated bimonthly meetings to encourage the sharing of best practices and to develop solutions around tough issues. I devised actionable programs, contests, and promotions that quickly impacted the business in Pepsi's central region. I developed a "Partnership 2000" program targeted to high school and university students to drive soft drink consumption, and, once approved, I had all of the needed vending equipment and supplies in place to execute the program in a quick two and one-half months.

I organized a team effort to sell to Trans World Airlines (TWA), a Coca-Cola account, and presented a plan to assist TWA in filling passenger seats through a joint program, which guaranteed $1million in upfront ticket purchases by PepsiCo for each year of the five-year agreement. I helped negotiate an acceptable pricing program with the Cleveland and St. Louis bottlers to help support the TWA agreement.

When an opportunity to advance stalled due to multiple reengineering changes within the Pepsi organization, I was recruited to Altria, enticed by the increased technology, resources, market information, and data available. (Philip Morris USA rarely hires from the outside.) I moved to Chicago as a district manager responsible for five unit managers, two senior account managers, and twenty territory sales managers in the greater Chicago area. I also had responsibility for the successful management of our relations with our district's large retail accounts, including Jewel/Osco, Dominicks, Mobil Oil, and Gas Center accounts. With total sales over $200 million for the Marlboro, Benson & Hedges, Virginia Slims, Merit, Basic, Cambridge, and Alpine brands, I was brought in on the heels of the famous "Marlboro Friday" and its drastic price adjustment. I needed to jumpstart the business with a strategy that would put Philip Morris foremost in the minds of the consumer with the right price to help promote value to the end user.

My accomplishments included the following:

- Reorganizing the sales team and delivering a training program on Development Dimensions International's Interaction Management Program, which promoted collaboration skills to be used both internally and externally.

- Designing a program and plan to increase revenue through the improved usage of flex and merchandising dollars to lower the price, as opposed to using both to promote the product, which was already getting national attention.

Eleven months later, in November 1994, I was promoted to director of trade marketing, one of five in the country, and moved to Philip Morris's New York City headquarters. I oversaw the distribution of marketing programs and information, merchandising equipment, and installation programs for the Southwestern Region (Texas, Missouri, Mississippi, Tennessee, Arkansas, New Mexico, Iowa, Kansas, and Nebraska). Major accounts included Kroger, Stop & Go Mobil Oil, and HEB, plus the management of four trade marketing managers and ten section logistics managers.

I was quick to institute many key programs, including the following:

- An enhanced process to track merchandising fixtures by types and inventory and established an electronic ordering process to help facilitate customer display needs in a timely and organized manner.
- Eliminated the adversarial relationship between field sales and trade marketing to promote improved fund allocation, productivity, and greater understanding of trade marketing's role and capabilities. I instituted a

"Coverage Plus" program that encouraged my managers to work in the field, partnering with and supporting trade marketing efforts and contributing analysis and programs where needed.

In February 1996, I was promoted to section sales director (one of twenty-two in the country) and moved to Indianapolis, Indiana. I was responsible for PM USA sales in the states of Indiana, Kentucky, Ohio, and West Virginia. Major accounts included SuperAmerica, Thornton Oil, Kroger, Winn-Dixie, Marsh Supermarkets, Village Pantry, Johnson Oil, McLane Convenience Stores Distribution Company, Eby Brown, and Richmond Masters. My sales organization included three district sales managers, one section operations manager, fourteen unit managers, eight senior account managers, two section fixture logistics managers, two sales development associates, and sixty-eight territory sales managers.

I experienced many accomplishments by reorganizing my team and decreasing four districts to three through strong management and business training and refocusing my organization's efforts on the customer.

My specific accomplishments were as follows:

- Developed a section business game plan that resulted in a 7.2 percent increase in sales, a +1.45 share points gain, and improved partnerships with key retailers in 1997.
- Developed and launched a business measurement ranking system called the "Section Barometer." Key

measures include share growth, sales call productivity, pay for performance of all merchandising programs, and program execution. My idea for a Section Barometer was introduced by PM USA senior management on a national level to track section sales directors' and region vice presidents' performances. In 1997, my section was ranked third out of twenty-two sections in an overall composite rating of eight various business measures.

- Developed a "Retail Interaction Management" training program to assist all members of my sales organization to improve relations with their customers.

- Convinced major convenience store chains to highlight an everyday low retail price on cartons of Marlboro. In most convenience stores, 90 percent of cigarettes are sold by the pack, while 10 percent of category sales are sold by the carton. The pack/carton sales mix at supermarkets and tobacco stores is just the opposite of convenience stores.

- Promoted cartons versus packs at the major convenience store chains to extend a valued price on Marlboro for a longer time as a result of slower usage of flex and merchandising funds offered by PM USA. I named the program "The Marlboro Carton Advantage Program." Many of my large retail customers experienced sharp increases in sales and profits as a result of implementing this program.

- To insure that my entire organization was informed about our overall priorities, I developed and launched an internal staff-only newsletter called the "Section

Connection" to improve communication of success stories, priorities, and best practices.

- During my tenure as section sales director, I promoted eleven team members to greater responsibilities and hired seven summer interns and eleven new territory sales managers from Indiana University and Howard University.

In 1998, American Express recruited me to join their corporate services division as vice president and general manager (VPGM) of the Western region (one of five VPGMs in the United States in 1998/one of four VPGMs in 1999). As VPGM, I was responsible for managing a staff of seventy-seven employees, including a direct staff of four sales directors and three account development directors.

My team was responsible for selling the American Express corporate travel and entertainment credit card, corporate purchasing card, corporate travel services, and AMEX fully integrated and automated management tools to middle-market corporate clients, which included companies with revues from $1 million to just under $1 billion in gross sales. The Western region represented more than 37 percent of the middle-market division's sales volume at $1.9 billion.

I quickly learned the corporate travel, purchasing, and expense management business and made solid contributions to the company. As a result of my leadership and ability to mobilize my sales and account development organizations, my region successfully acquired more than 2,000 new corporate accounts and exceeded its 1998 sales volume target by 6.3 percent.

During a national meeting in January 1998, I challenged my team to lead the country in sales volume. As a result of the region's fine results, the Western region ended 1998 ranked second out of five regions in delivering sales results against targets.

I collaborated with my staff to develop solid business measures and expectations. I launched a new performance measurement program called "Middle Market Metrics and Measures." The key measures monitored by Middle Market Metrics and Measures were weekly appointments per sales manager, weekly prospect telephone calls per sales manager, average accounts sold per week per sales manager, and pipeline management improvement. Middle Market Metrics and Measures generated region-wide understanding of the region's performance against volume and productivity objectives.

As a result of improved measurement of performance, the region experienced an increase in weekly appointments from an average of four to six, a 26 percent increase in the number of qualified clients in the sales pipeline, and led the country in signings per sales manager with 53.8 new signings per sales manager.

To improve my managers' skills in performance management and interaction management, I facilitated the Development Dimensions International Interaction Management Program for my direct management staff, and it led to improved collaboration and performance management in the region.

Another factor that led to my region's success was my personal initiative to challenge my organization to leverage and utilize the AMEX Value Proposition. With many competitors in the market offering rebates and lower prices for their services, I successfully mobilized the efforts of my management team to help my entire organization leverage the powerful technological automation, reporting, and consulting offered by AMEX. I personally led the effort to sell Safeway, a large retail supermarket chain located in Northern California, the American Express Fully Integrated Travel Program. I convinced Safeway executives that purchasing AXI would improve their employees' compliance with their travel policy and thereby reduce their travel and entertainment expenses by more than 10 percent, resulting in a projected $500,000 in savings. This initiative not only solidified AMEX's relationship with Safeway, it also provided a successful best practice for clients throughout my region.

During the fourth quarter of 1998, I executed a middle-market reengineering initiative called "Organization Effectiveness." As a result of this initiative, I successfully upgraded my management team with directors who had stronger leadership experience and skills, which led to improved operating results.

I provided solid contributions as a "VPGM Champion" on several key initiatives. I "championed" the 1998 Middle Market Incentive Task Force. As a result of my leadership of the Incentive Task Force, the 1999 Middle Market Division Sales Compensation Program was revised and enhanced. Key enhancements included an improved focus on driving new revenues through the Corporate Purchasing Card Program, improved performance standards and criteria for premium compensation kickers, and an improved formula for developing targets that were supported by market penetration.

During the fourth quarter of 1998, I was appointed as the VPGM Champion for Learning and Development. I quickly worked with the Learning and Development Department to develop a "Preparing for Success/Director Orientation Program." This national program was designed to provide all newly appointed sales and account development directors training on the fundamentals of strategic planning. I personally developed a module called "The American Express Middle Market Game Plan Model."

As a result of my personal development of a facilitator's guide and train the trainer program for the AMEX Game Plan Model, all the VPGMs of the middle market division learned how to facilitate the program. This program represented the first training program that was facilitated by VPGMs in the division of AMEX Middle Market. The program was launched in January 1999, and all its participants offered outstanding feedback. My development of the American Express Middle Market Game Plan Model greatly contributed to the division's increase in sales revenue, improvement in organizational productivity, and enhancement in manager effectiveness.

My success as a vice president and general manager for the Western region led to my promotion to vice president and general manager of the Middle Market Consulting Services Group in July 1999. The Middle Market Consulting Services Group (MMCSG) had a similar function as a traditional trade marketing department. The MMCSG had a staff of forty-one team members, encompassing four directors and one senior manager who reported to me. The key areas of focus for the MMCSG included client acquisition and new channel development, client loyalty and expansion development, strategic planning and business analysis, e-commerce and new product development, and incentive, rewards, and recognition development.

I quickly collaborated with my directors to develop a new vision for the MMCSG. The "MMCSG Vision" resulted in the development of five key initiatives for developing the middle-market segment in 2000. Major initiatives I led included the following:

- **Market Segmentation Study**: This study determined that American Express had a 32 percent penetration in the upper tier accounts and about 10 percent in the lower-tier, highly transactional accounts, which clearly documented evidence for long-term growth opportunities.

- **Project Surge**: I commissioned an alliance between AMEX's Middle Market Division and ETI Sales & Support to accelerate the sales cycle and to capture enhanced marketing intelligence on targeted prospective customers across the country. ETI Sales & Support is a professional, business-to-business-lead generation and business to business telemarketing company with an expertise to generate pre-qualified prospects for large, national field sales organizations. This partnership with ETI Sales & Support reduced thousands of hours per week in telephone prospecting by the field sales force and delivered a projected 100 percent increase in client signings per sales representative across the country.

- **Project Fast Forward**: Rapid expansion of corporate purchasing card charge volume through a centralized account-relationship management team.
- **E-Client Forums**: Developed and launched a full schedule of Client Forums to be facilitated over the Internet to build scale and maximum coverage of acquisition opportunities. E-Client Forums involved presentations of the AMEX Value Proposition for the corporate card and corporate purchasing card.
- **Sales Force Incentive Compensation 2000**: Developed and launched twenty-four improved sales and account-development compensation programs for year 2000, involving more aggressive minimum performance to target for payment. An incentive-design team was formed from field representatives to ensure alignment of goals and overall support of the new compensation plan.

I effectively mobilized my staff and resources against the above 1999-2000 initiatives to drive a projected 20 percent growth rate in corporate card charge volume and a 200 percent growth rate in corporate purchasing card volume. I effectively secured the endorsement of all the VPGMs of each region for these initiatives, and I gained their commitment for effective execution of each initiative.

After a seventeen-year tenure, I left the good life of being a Fortune 500 corporate executive in 2000 to carry out my journey in the technology startup world, as well as to get involved in politics and public service. It was a rough decade ahead, filled with many learning experiences that prepared me for my current role of being an economic development expert.

During my corporate career, I was fortunate to learn the following *Cut the Crap and Close the Gap* management approach fundamentals:

DON'T WAIT TO BE RECRUITED BY A MENTOR, RECRUIT A MENTOR

I am a direct product of my parents, who were positive role models. Each of my siblings is a role model, as well. I was also blessed to be exposed to a wonderful grandfather, my mother's father, as well as wonderful uncles and aunts who were very powerful role models and mentors.

During the last thirty-plus years in my business career, I have been fortunate to be exposed to very positive and successful role models in the business world. One of my favorite role models and mentors was Barry Hopkins, a former senior executive at Philip Morris USA. Barry adopted me as a protégé, showed me the ropes, and talked to me in ways that encouraged me to quickly act upon his advice. Barry is still my mentor today, and I'll never forget his tremendous encouragement and advice. When I hear from him, it brings me powerful joy and happiness.

Identifying and aligning yourself with a positive role model is like purchasing a franchise business. A role model offers you an example of success. A role model offers a roadmap and is willing to share different and unique ways to solve problems and achieve success.

To achieve maximum fulfillment and success, we cannot wait for a positive role model to volunteer to be our mentors. Successful people recruit positive role models as mentors, nurture these relationships, and call upon their role models and mentors for help, advice, encouragement, and direction. Successful people know that a successful mentoring relationship generates mutual happiness for the mentor and the protégé.

MINIMIZE YOUR EXPOSURE TO NEGATIVE PEOPLE

The old saying, "Birds of a feather flock together," is absolutely true. Another old saying that I live by is, "We are the average of our five best friends," which I have also found to be true. The people we surround ourselves with impact our lives enormously. Our first surroundings, comprised of parents and siblings, are critical. If our family life is challenged early on, our probability for success is negatively impacted.

Negative people are people who see no need in trying and are often more comfortable in making up excuses for their own failures versus owning their mistakes and challenges. Negative people do not encourage others and are often more critical than positive. Negative people can drain us of our ability to see opportunity and the future. With positive people, the glass is always half full; with negative people, the glass is always half empty.

MAKE A HABIT OUT OF BEING HAPPY

This does not mean being a phony or a fake. This does not mean never being able to cry when you are sad. Making a habit out of being happy is being disciplined and mature enough to realize that life is not always easy and that we build our greatest capabilities when we successfully confront our challenges. Making a habit out of being happy is having the discipline to always try to see the positives in every situation, good or bad.

As I mentioned earlier, my father used to say, "It's always darkest before the dawn." What my father meant is that even when we are faced with the most difficult of challenges, brighter days are on the way if we remain committed to achieving our desired objectives.

My father was always enthusiastic about life. He had no choice because he'd lost his mother when he was only ten years old. He had to be a man at that point, but he always believed his mother was watching over him and that she wanted him to behave, be a success, and be responsible.

FIRE UP YOUR MENTAL AND PHYSICAL HEALTH

Nothing is more important. If we don't have our mental or physical health, we cannot accomplish anything. Our mental and physical health are more important than our most precious loved ones. Our loved ones and dear friends need us to be healthy, mentally and physically. This means that we must refrain from those mental and physical things that limit our longevity and embrace those things that extend our longevity.

It's easier said than done, but we must adhere to a daily mental and physical diet. We must exercise our minds and our bodies to keep ourselves vibrant, alert, and prepared for life's battles. We have more power over our mental and physical health than we give ourselves credit. Successful people are mentally and physically fit, active, and healthy.

PLAN YOUR WORK AND WORK YOUR PLAN

The adage, "Most people don't plan to fail; they fail to plan," is very true. My father always had a plan to send all of his children to college. He knew he needed to make and save a lot of money to finance this venture. To generate the finances required to send us all to college, he worked at the post office, raised crops and animals on our farm for the market, and worked as a waiter for private parties for many of the race horse farm owners in Lexington.

It was not easy, but he accomplished his goal of sending us all to college, and none of us ever had a large, burdensome college loan to pay off. My father often challenged me to work hard and sacrifice today for a brighter future. He forever reminded me that my hard work on the farm would pay off by generating enough revenue for him to finance my education at Howard.

I did not fully understand the power of my father's plan until I arrived at Howard's Student Accounts office to pay for my tuition with a certified check. That day, I learned that my father had planned his work and worked his plan. I also learned that if I plan my work and work my plan, I can stand in the short line of life. Successful people plan their work and work their plans!

KNOW THE DESIRED VS. THE ACTUAL PERFORMANCE OF YOUR BUSINESS AT ALL TIMES

Knowing the status of our personal financial health at all times is as simple as knowing how much we have in our bank accounts. Understanding our commitments, our strengths, and weaknesses and knowing what we are going to do today and tomorrow to improve our own lives, makes our lives better. It's impossible to cut the crap and close the gap if we don't know where we stand at all times.

Knowing your company's desired vs. actual performance at all times requires discipline and a brave look at reality. Knowing the status of the performance of our business at all times means we have assessed our operation, our business results, and our team members who operate our business to give us an idea of what we need to do tomorrow to make our business run better.

Successful business owners, managers, and executives are driven by a deep desire to know the status of the performance of their business every day, and they adhere to a quantitative dashboard of simple, easy-to-understand metrics that measure their ongoing performance.

STRATEGICALLY DISTRIBUTE PRECIOUS RESOURCES

From the start of my career as manager of Coleman Crest until today, my days are filled with distributing precious resources, like time, money, staff, office supplies, promotional resources, and other items crucial to my operations. Managing the allocation and distribution of these precious resources can make or break our efforts at delivering actual performance results that far exceed desired performance expectations.

EVANGELIZE YOUR VISON AND EXPECTATIONS TO YOUR TEAM ON A CONTINUOUS BASIS

Successful evangelists realize that followers need continuous encouragement and evangelism to adhere to their philosophy and ministry. As a successful manager and executive, I evangelize by providing direction in verbal, as well as written, format. Time moves fast, and people need to hear and understand a simple message about what is expected of them and how they are performing versus a desired set of performance metrics and objectives.

WE ARE ONLY AS STRONG AS OUR WEAKEST TEAM MEMBER, SO CONTINUOUSLY IMPROVE INDIVIDUAL AND ORGANIZATIONAL SKILLS AND CAPABILITIES

This means developing individual team member's skills and performance so that the organization has a strong bench and can deliver long-term results. Organizations are only as strong as their weakest team members, so it is crucial to build an organization that is constantly learning and growing and improving its impact in the market. Market leaders in any business sector are those organizations that experience the least employee turnover and are known for retaining and developing highly skilled and capable managers and employees who embrace the organization's vision of success. All of the Fortune 500 companies I've worked for meet this incredibly high standard.

CLOSE THE GAP TAKEAWAYS:

- Preparation + Timing = Incredible Success
- A simple set of easy to understand performance metrics will drive record results.
- If we surround ourselves with happy people, we will be happy. If we surround ourselves with negative people, we will be negative.
- A good strong work ethic and a positive personality are worth more than good grades.

CHAPTER 8

THE LAST DANCE

Cut the Crap Principle 8: Live like you are dying.
All that counts is to love, be loved, and leave a legacy.

 othing is permanent, including life. The average person lives a brief seventy-nine years. Time goes by fast, and our lives are full of constant change. No job, no relationship, no material is permanent. We must enjoy our family members, friends, and associates as much as possible while we have them because life is so precious, delicate, and short. During my brief life, I've lost my parents, a grandfather, twelve uncles and aunts, and several friends and mentors. My thirty-plus year career journey has exposed me to more than seventeen jobs, thirteen employers, and more than thirty bosses.

I've concluded that life offers no resting place. It constantly evolves and changes. Successful people don't live in the past, and they are not preoccupied with the future. They live their best lives now and make the most out of every moment.

My parents were married for nearly forty years until my father's death on December 17, 1989. The passing of my father represented one of the saddest days in my life. My father suffered from leukemia, but he never gave up on living. When the doctors told him he had cancer, he said, "Does that mean I have to quit smoking?" His doctor replied, "Mr. Coleman, that won't be necessary." My father turned to my mother and said, "Cleo, let's get out of here."

Even when cancer had ravaged his body and left him weighing less than 100 pounds, he always saw life in a positive way. The glass was always half full, and he accepted death as being a part of life. My father is the most courageous man I have ever known. I've met hundreds of powerful CEOs and elected officials, but none of them stand up to my father's courage, internal strength, and desire to succeed.

During Daddy's final days, one of his favorite nieces, Sarah, came to visit him from Dayton, Ohio. Sarah asked him, "Uncle Bud, how are you doing"? Daddy simply said, "I'm doing fine.

I'm just dying." With that, Sarah started to cry, and Daddy ended up consoling her during her final visit with him.

On a cold Sunday afternoon, December 17, 1989, Daddy was sitting in his favorite chair in his bedroom. Like many times before and during his illness, Cupcakes would help him from his chair to their bed so he could go to sleep. This ritual had become one of my parents' most intimate forms of affection. On this particular day, Daddy said, "Cleo, my body has had it. I don't think I'm going to last much longer." Cupcakes responded, "Oh, Bud, you are going to be fine. You have many years ahead. Let me help you to the bed." She was in denial about my father's impending death; she had become used to him being sick and believed it was just another one of "those days."

She wasn't frightened or alarmed. She reached out to clinch his hands to pull him up from his chair, had him to place his feet on top of her feet, wrapped her arms warmly around his body, and walked him one step at a time, face to face, till they got to their bed. When she laid Daddy on in his back on their bed, she knew something special was happening. She said she felt his spirit begin to leave his body. Daddy's favorite dog and best friend, Oscar, a little reddish-brown dachshund, would always lie under the bed when my father was in it, but this time, Oscar began to make a very different and curious sound, as if he were yelling instead of barking. With all of this happening, Cupcakes looked closely into Daddy's eyes, and my father silently stared at the woman he'd deeply loved for more than forty years for one last time. Then he was gone. He was at peace, free of excruciating pain and eternally at rest.

Even though Daddy had passed away right before her eyes, at that moment, Cupcakes simply laid beside him on their bed and hugged him saying, "Oh, Bud, I love you so much," and began to closely massage and hug his body as she prayed for his soul. It was their special time together and the end to their last dance, a milestone for both of them, an ending just as sweet as their beginning.

Somehow it was a miracle that my oldest brother, Bubba, was already there for a visit with my parents on this incredible day. Bubba somehow found the courage and the strength to console my mother, and he began the painful process of calling all of Daddy's siblings, Uncle Ben and Aunt Sister, and a host of our other relatives and friends to tell them that Daddy had died. Bubba was the right person to be with my mother and father on that day—I'm sure it was the Lord's will for him to be present. Bubba is one of the most mature, quiet, warm, and strong men I've known.

When Daddy died, my mother became the sole custodian of Coleman Crest Farm. For the remainder of her life, until her death in 2002, she lived on the farm with her dogs, and she cared for our farm and our family home.

CLOSE THE GAP TAKEAWAYS:

- While death is the common equalizer, we don't have to be afraid to take it head-on till the end.
- We have the power to choose between happiness and sadness in the face of death.
- Life doesn't have to end at death; we get to determine our own legacy by how we care for others and how we

contribute to society and our community during our brief time on Earth.

- The human spirit is not stored at the cemetery. It's stored in the hearts of the people we touch along the way.

CHAPTER 9

A MOTHER'S FAREWELL

Cut the Crap Principle 9: I thought the light had gone from my life forever, but it isn't so, because until you've lived in life's deepest valleys, you can't ever know how majestic it is to be at the top of the mountain.

During my career as a Fortune 500 executive, I invited my parents to visit each city where I resided, including Washington, DC, Philadelphia, New York, Chicago, Cleveland, and San Francisco. Saying thanks to them while they were still alive proved to be the most exciting time of my life. I'm glad I took advantage of every chance I had to visit them and to enable them to travel to the many cities where I lived. It seems that time passed by very quickly, and my time with my parents went by so suddenly.

In 2001, Cupcakes was diagnosed with lung cancer. The doctor told me she had anywhere from a year to a year and a half to live. I was stunned by the news from her doctor, and it made me quickly prepare for this incredible loss. Cupcakes fought valiantly. She remained proud and very strong throughout her entire fight with cancer.

In the fall of 2002, I visited with Cupcakes at her apartment at The Lafayette, an assisted living community in Lexington, Kentucky. During my visit with her, she told me she was tired, was not up to fighting any longer, and was not willing to go through another round of chemotherapy. I did my best to immediately relieve her. I told her it was okay not to fight any longer and that she did not need to endure any more pain from chemotherapy. I told Cupcakes that she had been the best mother in the whole wide world and that my brothers and sisters and I would be just fine and that she had done a wonderful job of raising us. Because of her, I said, we could take care of ourselves and our families. Instantly, Cupcakes was relieved. She smiled and stared at me as if all her pain had been released from her body. Little did I know that this would be the last time I would see Cupcakes alive.

On the clear, cold morning of December 7, 2002, I was flying to Lexington for what I considered my last chance to see Cupcakes. During a stopover in Pittsburgh to transfer to my final flight to Lexington, I checked my voicemail messages only to find that my dear sister Ruth had called to inform me that Cupcakes was slipping away and to call her. I called Ruth right at that moment, and she informed me that Cupcakes had just passed away. Our brother Bubba had been there with her. I was relieved for Cupcakes because I knew she was no longer in pain. Now, she was finally at peace and in heaven with my father and her Lord.

I was concerned about Bubba because he had been with my father at the time of his death and now he'd been with my mother when she died. I knew this must have been a very heavy burden for him to carry.

When I hung up the phone after Ruth informed me about Cupcakes's passing, I instantly became an orphan. For forty-two years, Cupcakes had allowed me to be her little man, her protégé. Now I had to carry on my life without her physical presence. After I called my wife and her mother to tell them the news, I called my good friend and college roommate, Mike Smart, to tell him and to just talk. Miraculously, Mike answered my call on the first ring. I could barely contain myself enough to tell him my sad news about the loss of my mother. I remember it like it was yesterday. Mike said, "I'm so sorry, Doe, I'm so sorry." It was the first time that I had cried about my mother's death and the giant loss that I was facing.

Mike is a good friend and special brother that I can confide in on any issue. He can be counted on for confidential and wise advice. We were good friends and roommates at Howard. We were both raised by powerful parents, and we both had a bunch of brothers and sisters. I used to tease Mike that he was a "Dough Boy." This is what my father used to call any man that was soft or too sensitive. Today we call each other Doe Boy, and I call his wife Mrs. Doe and Mike's daughter "Baby Doe." Doe is one of the most generous people I've ever met. He is generous to his family and friends and to strangers. He has supported every venture I've ever launched, including a dot-com I managed and my campaign for the New York State Assembly in 2006.

During a long walk through my neighborhood in Scarsdale, New York, after I had to close down Iguana Interactive, the dot-com that I tried to build in New York City, Mike turned to me and asked if I needed $50,000 or $100,000 as a loan until I got a new job. He was always willing to step in to offer help, even before I asked. I thank my mother again for the letter she sent Dr. Cheek because I would not have been blessed by having an angel like Mike in my life if she hadn't sent her letter.

During Cupcakes's eulogy, I spoke to the congregation that included family, friends, and my mother's former colleagues, as well as friends and staff at The Lafayette. I told Rev. Joe McDowell, Senior Pastor of Uttingertown Baptist Church, and the congregation that Cupcakes did not want me to tell the story about the letter she wrote to Dr. James Cheek, president of Howard, on my behalf. She had not wanted her friends and colleagues, Mrs. Virginia French or Mrs. Lilian Perkins, to think I was slow. I turned to Reverend Joe and told him that I wasn't slow. I'd just needed what every child in this world needs and that is "a mother's letter," and that is just what the Lord gave me through Cupcakes.

With all the success I have enjoyed since my mother wrote her letter nearly forty years ago, losing her continues to be devastating and very painful for me. Even after fifteen years, I mourn her loss every day. When I lost my mother, I felt as if the light had been taken from my life forever.

To cope with the pain and setback of losing Cupcakes, I read a lot of books. I recalled President Richard Nixon's farewell address to the nation when he mentioned that he had read about a young lawyer who resided in New York. President Nixon went on to explain that this young man had married a beautiful girl and that they had a lovely daughter, but then suddenly his wife died, and this is what the young man wrote in his diary that day:

> She was beautiful in face and form and lovelier still in spirit. As a flower she grew and as a fair young flower she died. Her life had been always in the sunshine. There had never come to her a single great sorrow. None ever knew her who did not love and revere her for her bright and sunny temper and her saintly unselfishness. Fair, pure and joyous as a maiden, loving, tender and happy as a young wife. When she had just become a mother, when her life seemed to be just begun and when the years seemed so bright before her, then by a strange and

terrible fate, death came to her. And when my heart's dearest died, the light went from my life forever.

The young man who wrote this diary entry was Theodore Roosevelt. He was in his early twenties. He thought the light had gone from his life forever—but he went on. He not only became President of the United States, but he also served his country after leaving office. President Roosevelt was always in the arena, tempestuous, strong, sometimes wrong, sometimes right, but he became a great man while facing many setbacks and personal challenges.

President Nixon further explained during his very sad farewell and final speech to the American people:

We think sometimes when things happen that don't go the right way, we think that when you don't pass the bar exam the first time—I happened to, but I was just lucky; I mean my writing was so poor the bar examiner said, "We have just gotta let the guy through." We think that when someone dear to us dies, we think that when we lose an election, we think that when we suffer a defeat, that all is ended. We think, as T.R. said, that the light had left his life forever.

Not true. It's only a beginning—always. The young must know it; the old must know it. It must always sustain us because the greatness comes not when things go always good for you, but the greatness comes when you are really tested, when you take some knocks, some disappointments, when sadness comes; because only if you've been in the deepest valley can you ever know how magnificent it is to be on the highest mountain.

Every day, I think about my parents. They gave me an incredible foundation from which to confront any challenge, and they provided me the love and direction that I have relied on to be successful. They were precious role models, and I'll always rely on their advice and wise counsel to take on any challenge I face for the rest of my life.

Hoping to become just like my parents, Cleo and Samuel Coleman, I will continue in their footsteps, conducting missionary work that is based on love, creating value for others, and caring for my fellow neighbors in this country and throughout the world.

CLOSE THE GAP TAKEAWAYS:

- Letting go of our loved ones can be the best gift we can ever give them.
- Losing a loved one can empower us to do great things for other people, in memory of our loved one.
- Living a life of urgency is important because life is so short and temporary; never put off what you should and can do today.
- The belief of favor can enable us to move mountains. The incredible efforts to seize the moment by my great-grandfather, grandparents, and my parents directly led to my success and sustainability. I am living proof of favor.

ABOUT THE AUTHOR

Economic developer, consummate deal maker, Fortune 500 Executive, results-oriented business executive, high-energy motivational communicator, Kentucky hog farmer, and author.

From his family's farm in Lexington, Kentucky, to Wall Street, Jim Coleman has delivered stellar results over the last thirty-four years with Oscar Mayer & Co., Pepsi Cola Company,

Altria Corporation, American Express, several entrepreneurial ventures, and several government entities, including the New York State Senate and two of America's most wealthy counties.

As a senior sales and marketing executive, Jim has negotiated hundreds of complex deals with large, multibillion dollar clients in the meat packing, soft drink, tobacco, financial services, and high-tech sectors, which have all led to over $10 billion in sales as a direct result of his personal effort and leadership.

Jim achieved the American Dream early in life. He purchased his first home at the age of twenty-five in Lanham, Maryland. He became a senior executive in a large Fortune 500 global corporation by the time he was thirty-eight. He acquired millions of dollars in real estate by the time he was forty-three, and today, as a highly sought after motivational speaker, he is committed to helping others achieve the American Dream.

Jim is committed to serving others, making a big impact, and leaving a legacy that his parents, Cleo and Sam Coleman, would be proud of. According to Jim, America offers an abundance of unlimited opportunities because the American Dream is real and because America remains the world's best hope for prosperity for the common man or woman.

All of Jim's personal accomplishments have been achieved because, early in his life, he embraced the precious wisdom and advice of his parents, Cleo and Sam Coleman, and, later, he learned from the many generous Fortune 500 executives, elected officials, and pastors who've mentored him and, even at times, tolerated his deficiencies and weaknesses and made him a better man.

Cut the Crap and Close the Gap offers a management approach and a practical guide for success on how family farmers, small business owners, Fortune 500 executives, and managers, as well as not-for-profit executive directors, can exceed desired operating results for their organizations. It's filled with a wide selection of stories that are linked to practical advice and key learnings that can be applied to any situation by the reader.

Jim was raised on his family's farm, Coleman Crest, in Lexington, Kentucky, which was originally purchased by his great-grandfather, James Coleman, on March 27, 1888, for $1,200 after he and his family had tilled the farm as slaves. Jim owns Coleman Crest Farm today. Jim's incredible business success and travels have taken him from a Kentucky farming community, called Uttingertown in Fayette County, to Wall Street to Silicon Valley to Beijing, China, and to the nation's capitol.

Jim is a proud graduate of Howard University with a B.A. in Economics. During his tenure at Howard, Jim was elected President of the Liberal Arts Student Council and was inducted into the Who's Who Among Students at Colleges and Universities by Dr. James Cheek, President of Howard University.

Jim is a certified management training facilitator in Development Dimensions International's management and development training programs and he is a 2014 graduate of the World Wide College of Auctioneering.

Morgan James
Speakers Group

We connect Morgan James published
authors with live and online events
and audiences whom will benefit
from their expertise.

Morgan James makes all of our titles available
through the Library for All Charity Organization.

www.LibraryForAll.org

CPSIA information can be obtained
at www.ICGtesting.com
Printed in the USA
BVOW08s1637210118
505479BV00001B/4/P